BLACK ✦ STARS

AFRICAN AMERICAN TEACHERS

CLINTON COX

JIM HASKINS, GENERAL EDITOR

John Wiley & Sons, Inc.
New York • Chichester • Weinheim • Brisbane • Singapore • Toronto

This book is printed on acid-free paper. ♾

Published by John Wiley & Sons, Inc.
Published simultaneously in Canada
Design and production by Navta Associates, Inc.

This publication is designed to provide accurate and authoritative information in regard
to the subject matter covered. It is sold with the understanding that the publisher is not
engaged in rendering professional services. If professional advice or other expert assistance
is required, the services of a competent professional person should be sought.

Library of Congress Cataloging-in-Publication Data:

Cox, Clinton.
    African American teachers / Clinton Cox.
        p. cm. — (Black stars series)
    Includes bibliographical references (p.) and index.
    ISBN 0-471-24649-2 (cloth : alk. paper)
    1. Afro-American teachers—Biography.   2. Afro-Americans—Education—History.
    I. Title.   II. Black stars (New York, N.Y.)

LA2311 .C69 2000
371.1'0092'2—dc21
[B]
                                                                    99-055356

Printed in the United States of America
10 9 8 7 6 5 4 3 2 1

CONTENTS

INTRODUCTION

✦

In each decade from the earliest days of this nation's history to the present, committed African American men and women have dedicated their lives to spreading the gift of knowledge. No obstacles could prevent them from teaching and learning. This book gives you a chance to meet these black stars.

"Knowledge unfits a child to be a slave," Frederick Douglass discovered one day while still a child. "I instinctively assented to the proposition, and from that moment I understood the direct pathway between slavery and feedom."[1]

In the North, members of the free black population often pooled their meager resources and built schools for their children, who were usually banned from schools for whites. Without education, the dream of freedom could not survive.

There were people such as Daniel Coker, who escaped from slavery and became a teacher at Baltimore's African School in 1802. There was Susie King Taylor, who followed her husband when he enlisted in the all-black First South Carolina Volunteers in the Civil War, and spent countless hours teaching the black soldiers to read and write.

In the first half of the twentieth century, there were inspiring educators like Mary McLeod Bethune, who rode "interminable miles of dusty roads on my old bicycle" to plead for the nickels and dimes that enabled her to start Bethune-Cookman College in Daytona Beach, Florida.[2]

And now there are such teachers as Dr. Mae Jemison, a former astronaut and now a college professor. Dr. Jemison is developing programs aimed at bringing quality science teaching to students today.

"Knowledge is power, ay, and liberty and equality too," declared Boston resident Thomas Smith in 1850, arguing for the right of black children to attend school.[3]

By learning about some of the countless African American men and women who have dedicated their lives to spreading knowledge, we can also learn much about the history of our country and ourselves.

PART ONE

◆

THE EARLY YEARS

BENJAMIN
BANNEKER

(1731–1806)

In the decades before the Revolutionary War, which resulted in the founding of the United States, it was widely believed that black people were incapable of intellectual achievement.

Slavery and racial discrimination were justified by the argument that black people were no more capable of learning than were animals such as horses and cows.

Then along came a man who challenged these assumptions "with the fire of his intellect," one nineteenth-century historian declared, forcing Thomas Jefferson and others to question their belief in black inferiority.[1]

The man's name was Benjamin Banneker, and there is probably no better example of the desire to learn and to teach others than that shown by him throughout his life.

Banneker was not a teacher in the usual sense, with a classroom full of students. Instead, he taught mathematics, astronomy, history,

- ✦ **Mathematics** is the science and study of numbers and how they operate.
- ✦ **Astronomy** is the science and study of the stars, moon, and planets.

5

and other subjects by publishing his knowledge in pamphlets that came out once a year.

Born to free black parents, Mary and Robert Banneker, on a farm near the Patapsco River in Baltimore County, Maryland, Benjamin Banneker had deep roots on two continents and a deep understanding of the meaning of freedom.

Benjamin had an English grandmother, Molly Welsh. In about 1683 she had been found guilty of stealing milk from a farmer. In fact, she had accidentally knocked over a pail of milk, but the mistake was costly. Molly was shipped to the American colonies as an indentured servant to pay for her crime.

After toiling for seven years on a tobacco plantation in Maryland, Molly had earned her freedom. She then bought a small farm and two slaves. One of the slaves was a man named Bannka or Banneka, who said he was the son of an African chieftain.

Within three years, Molly freed Bannka. In spite of strict laws against interracial marriages, Molly and Bannka married and had a daughter, Mary Banneky ("daughter of Bannka or Banneka"). The name was later changed to Banneker.

When Mary fell in love with a slave named Robert, her parents bought his freedom so the young couple could marry. Having no surname, Robert took his wife's family name as his own. Benjamin was the first of the four children they would have.

Benjamin's first teacher was his grandmother, Molly. She taught him to read and write by using a Bible she had imported from England. Benjamin's mind was sharp, and he soon learned all that Molly had to teach, so she sent him to a one-room school near her farm.

As he grew older, Benjamin had to work full time on his father's farm, but he continued to educate himself for the rest of his life. Few books were available at the time (Benjamin could not afford a book of his own until he was thirty-two years old), but he managed to borrow books and teach himself literature, history, and mathematics.

DIVING INTO BOOKS

Benjamin Banneker went to a school that accepted both black and white students. It was open only during the winter months, when the children did not have to work on their parents' farms. The few years Benjamin spent there constituted the only formal education he ever received. Jacob Hall, one of Banneker's black classmates, said Benjamin showed little interest in fun and games. Instead, Hall recalled, "all his delight was to dive into his books."[2]

He was so good at mathematics that visitors came from far away with practical problems or brain-teasing puzzles for him to solve.

At age twenty-two, Banneker built a striking clock without ever having seen one. First, he studied the workings of a small watch, then used a pocket knife to carve each part of his clock from wood he had collected and carefully seasoned. He used metal parts only where they were absolutely needed. It was the first clock of its kind in the Maryland region.

Banneker enjoyed the mathematical challenge of calculating the proper ratio of the many gears, wheels, and other parts, then fitting them together to move in harmony. His clock operated for more than forty years, striking the hours of six and twelve. Visitors came from miles around to see the amazing achievement of this self-taught man.

One day, a friendly Quaker neighbor named George Ellicott lent Banneker a telescope, some other instruments, and several books on astronomy. From that moment on, the study of astronomy dominated Banneker's life. He often spent entire nights studying the stars, after working all day on the farm. Eventually, the Ellicott family bought part of Banneker's farm. They agreed to pay him enough money each year to live on, and thus enabled him to spend the last sixteen years of his life studying astronomy full time.

Banneker's studies progressed rapidly, and he began making all the calculations necessary for an almanac for the Delaware, Maryland, Pennsylvania, and Virginia regions. But his work was suddenly interrupted by a request from his neighbor, George Ellicott, to help survey a 10-square-mile area known as the Federal Territory (now Washington, D.C.). Congress had decided to build a new national capital there, and one of George Ellicott's cousins, Major Andrew Ellicott, was appointed by President George Washington to head the survey.

So it was that Banneker, at age sixty, was hired by Secretary of State Thomas Jefferson and spent several months in 1791 helping to lay out the capital. Thomas Jefferson had earlier claimed that black people lacked intellectual skills, and the arrival of Banneker as a member of the surveying team led to the following comment in the *Georgetown Weekly Ledger:*

"Some time last month arrived in this town Mr. Andrew Ellicott [*sic*] . . . He is attended by Benjamin Banniker [*sic*], an Ethiopian, whose abilities, as a surveyor, and an astronomer, clearly prove that Mr. Jefferson's concluding that race of men were void of mental endowments, was without foundation."[3]

Banneker spent several months making and recording astronomical observations, maintaining the field astronomical clock, and compiling other data required by Ellicott. This work made him more interested than ever in astronomy, and when he returned home, he spent countless nighttime hours at his telescope. And on many nights, instead of using the telescope, the old man wrapped himself in a blanket and lay in a field watching the stars until dawn.

During the day, he worked at astronomical calculations for each day of the coming year (1792), and completed the calculations in just a few weeks. At last he was ready to publish his precious almanac.

With the help of the abolition societies, the almanac—*Benjamin Banneker's Pennsylvania, Delaware, Maryland and Virginia Almanack and Ephemeris, for the Year of Our Lord, 1792; Being Bissextile, or Leap-Year, and the Sixteenth Year of American Independence, which commenced July 4, 1776* was published in Baltimore and was a huge success.

Many colonists owned Bibles, but an almanac was usually the only other book in their homes. An almanac contained a calendar with astronomical information about each day, such as the rising and setting of the sun and the moon, phases of the moon, positions of the planets, and other observations about nature.

This information was especially prized at a time when most Americans made their living from farming. They used the observations to try to determine the best time to plant and harvest their crops.

The first almanac sold in great numbers, and Banneker published one every year for the next four years. The almanacs brought him international fame. He used that fame to prove that African Americans were as capable as anyone of learning and teaching.

He sent a copy of his almanac to Thomas Jefferson, who was a slave owner, along with a letter denouncing slavery and pointing out "that one universal Father hath . . . endued us all with the same faculties . . ."[4]

Jefferson, apparently moved by Banneker's arguments against slavery and impressed by the almanac, sent a copy of it to his friend the

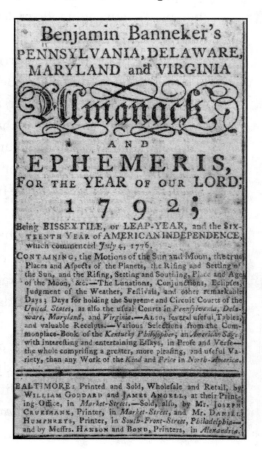

Benjamin Banneker's first almanac was published in 1792. It contained important information on the movements of the sun, moon, stars, and planets, and helped many farmers determine the best time to plant.

Marquis de Condorcet, secretary of the Academy of Sciences in Paris. Jefferson wrote, "I am happy to inform you that we have now in the United States a negro . . . who is a very respectable mathematician."[5]

Rarely leaving the farm where he was born, Benjamin Banneker used the power of his mind to discover things and give useful, accurate information to others throughout the almost seventy-five years of his life. Banneker continued to make his beloved calculations until a few months before his death on October 9, 1806.

CATHERINE (KATY)
FERGUSON

(C. 1779–1854)

Catherine Williams was born into slavery on a schooner sailing to New York City. At the time of her birth, her mother was being transported from Virginia to a new slave owner. Catherine, who would become known as Katy, was only eight years old when her mother was again sold. Katy never saw her again. The pain this separation caused may have been the reason she spent her adult life helping motherless children.

Katy was a deeply religious child. Though her mother could not read or write, she had taught Katy the Scriptures. And although Katy was a slave, she was allowed to attend New York City's Associate Reformed Church on Murray Street.

At age ten, Katy promised her owner that if he gave her her freedom, she would serve the Lord forever. Her owner, a Presbyterian elder, denied her request and continued to hold her in bondage. When Katy was sixteen, however, a sympathetic woman purchased her freedom for $200. Katy earned her living as a professional cake-maker for weddings and parties.

Katy's lifelong mission of helping poor children began four years later. Soon after her emancipation, she met and married a man named Ferguson and they had two children. Both children died in infancy, and her husband passed away before she was twenty. She never mentioned him again to friends or acquaintances. Instead, from that time on, she poured her heart into teaching and helping others.

Catherine Ferguson began helping the destitute children she saw near her home in lower Manhattan. There was little provision for educating the poor in the late eighteenth and early nineteenth centuries. Some were able to learn the rudiments of reading and writing by studying the Bible, and this is how Catherine began to teach her charges. Every Sunday, Ferguson "regularly collected the children in the neighborhood who are accustomed to run in the street on the Lord's day, into her house and got suitable persons to come and hear them say their catechism . . ."[1]

✦ **Catechism** is a set of religious lessons.

Ferguson supported her school with the money she earned from catering, and from her skill at cleaning fine laces. Sometime around 1814, the Reverend John Mitchell Mason of the Murray Street church invited her to relocate her activities to the church's lecture room. Katy accepted the offer, and from then on her school was known as the Murray Street Sabbath School. It was one of the earliest Sunday schools in New York City.

She continued to teach the Scriptures, while Reverend Mason provided her with assistants who taught the regular school subjects. The Sabbath School report for 1818—the only one that survives— shows that the school had eighty-eight students: twenty-six black and sixty-two white. Eleven of the black students were adults.

Ferguson also took both black and white homeless children into her own household, often going to the almshouses to seek them out. Some of the girls were unwed mothers. Treated as social outcasts, these girls had no place to go either during their pregnancies or after giving birth. Ferguson's organized effort was the first to help unwed mothers in New York City, and perhaps the first in the nation. A newspaper article published shortly after her death estimated that she had cared for twenty black and twenty-eight white children from the almshouses or from destitute parents.

Catherine Ferguson died of cholera in New York City on July 11, 1854. She was about seventy-five years old. Her efforts had become so widely known that an obituary was carried in the *New York Times*, and a short biographical article was published in the *New York Daily Tribune.*

She had spent the major part of her life serving poor people, especially the young, giving unknown numbers of them an education they would never have received otherwise. Her love and compassion also rescued scores from a life without hope.

In 1920, Ferguson's pioneering work as an educator and social worker was recognized when the Katy Ferguson Home for Unwed Mothers was opened in New York City. It was said to be the only home of its kind for black women in the United States.

In that same year, famed scholar W. E. B. Du Bois praised her in a collection of essays titled *Darkwater: Voices from Within the Veil*, as an example of that "human sympathy and sacrifice . . . characteristic of Negro womanhood."[2]

In words that summed up her labors of a lifetime and the gift of love she had so freely given, Du Bois wrote that Catherine (Katy) Ferguson had taken "the children of the streets of New York, white and black, to her empty arms, taught them, [and] found them homes . . ."[3]

DANIEL
COKER

(1780–1846)

Born a slave in Baltimore County, Maryland, to a black father and an indentured white mother, Daniel Coker became a fighter for African American freedom. Daniel was raised with his white half-brothers, who were children of his mother's first marriage.

Young Coker accompanied his white brothers to school as their servant. Quietly, he listened to the teachers' lessons. He could not be a regular student because it was illegal for anyone to educate a slave. But Daniel longed for education and freedom. He escaped to New York City while still a youth. There, he managed to obtain a good education, which was rare for an American of any color in that era. In addition, he was ordained a Methodist minister.

Now he was ready to return to Baltimore. But the move would have to be made in great secrecy because he was legally still a slave. He could be returned to slavery at any time, so going home was dangerous. Friends, however, soon raised enough money to help him buy his freedom. At this time, the Constitution of the United States

protected slavery and declared that African Americans were only three-fifths of a human being.

Courageous and compassionate, Coker ignored the dangers and began speaking out boldly against slavery and the treatment of black people throughout the United States. His fight for black freedom would last for the rest of his life. Like Benjamin Banneker, Coker would publish pamphlets to denounce slavery. One in particular, *A Dialogue Between a Virginian and an African Minister* (1810), became popular because it used arguments from the Bible.

SCHOOLS OF OUR OWN: THE PRINCE HALL STORY

In the early years, free African Americans had to start their own schools. Both blacks and whites in colonial America knew that educated people would struggle constantly to end slavery. For that reason, the education of slaves was banned almost everywhere, and the education of free black people was strongly discouraged.

The small free black population repeatedly demanded that their children be educated. In 1787, Prince Hall and several other African American parents wrote to the Massachusetts state legislature. They petitioned for "the education of our children which now receive no benefit from the free schools in the town of Boston, which we think is a great grievance, as by woeful experience we now feel the want of a common education. . . . We therefore pray your Honors that you would in your wisdom [make] some provision, . . . for the education of our dear children. . . ."[1] The legislators ignored Hall's request, so he helped establish a school in his own home and he hired two Harvard students as teachers.

The next year, Hall helped a black Baptist minister start a school for the children in his congregation, raising the necessary money from the contributions of black seamen along Boston's waterfront.

Free African Americans in other states also established schools. One was organized in Philadelphia by the Society of Free People of Color for Promoting the Instruction and School Education of Children of African Descent.

In 1802, Coker began teaching in the African School conducted by the Sharp Street Church in Baltimore. He taught there for the next fourteen years, combining his teaching with denunciations of slavery.

During those years at the Sharp Street Church, Coker and several other church leaders argued for the establishment of independent African Methodist churches. One of those leaders was Richard Allen, who had formed the first African Methodist Episcopal congregation several years earlier. In April 1816, Allen invited Coker and fourteen other Methodist leaders to a meeting in Philadelphia.

On April 9, 1816, these leaders and ministers formed a national organization called the African Methodist Episcopal Church. They elected Coker as their first bishop, but he declined the honor, which then went to Allen. When the African Methodist Episcopal Church in Baltimore established the African Bethel School, they turned to Coker again for help. This time he said yes. He spent the next four years as the school's teacher and manager.

Eager young students filled the newly created Baltimore Freedmen School.

In 1820, however, a new adventure captured the teacher's imagination. He became a missionary for the Maryland Colonization Society. The goal of colonization societies was to resettle free African Americans in other lands, especially Africa. Most black leaders thought the colonization schemes were a way to protect slavery and rid the United States of free black people. But some black Americans, including Coker, supported colonization because they believed whites would never treat them with dignity and equality in this country. So it was that Daniel Coker boarded a crowded ship bound for Africa. Coker kept a daily account of his voyage. He called it the *Journal of Daniel Coker, a Descendant of Africa, from the time of Leaving New York in the Ship Elizabeth, . . . on a Voyage for Sherbro, in Africa, in Company with Three Agents and about Ninety Persons of Colour . . . With an Appendix.*

Unfortunately, the three agents who accompanied the colonists soon died, leaving Coker with the sole responsibility of trying to establish a colony. He persevered and was commended by the managers of the colonization society for his "care, attention, and prudence, . . . in a time of great difficulty, and danger."[2]

Coker spent the rest of his life in Africa. He died in Freetown, Sierra Leone, leaving behind the church he had built on that African soil.

ALEXANDER LUCIUS
TWILIGHT

(1795–1857)

Alexander Lucius Twilight was born in Bradford, Vermont, to Ichabod and Mary Twilight. He was the third of the six children of this free black couple who apparently made their living by farming. At the time of Twilight's birth, almost 600 black people were living in Vermont.

Alexander was indentured to a local farmer until age twenty-one. He managed however to buy out the last year of his indenture and immediately set about obtaining an education while working to support himself. From 1815 to 1821, he completed secondary-school courses and the first two years of college-level courses at Randolph Academy in northeastern Vermont.

Alexander then enrolled in Middlebury College in Middlebury, Vermont, where he graduated in the summer of 1823 with a B.A. degree. He was the first known black graduate of an American college. Within weeks of receiving his degree, Twilight began the teaching career that would last for the rest of his life and touch the lives of thousands of young people.

He moved to Peru, New York, a small frontier community in the Adirondack Mountains, and taught there for four years. Twilight also found time to study theology, and was licensed to preach in 1827. He married Mercy Ladd Merrill and moved to Vergennes, Vermont, in 1828. For the next year, Twilight taught in the village and preached in neighboring towns on Sundays.

✦ **Theology** is the study of religion.

✦ **Philosophy** is the study of ideas.

✦ **Chemistry** is the study of how elements combine to make new compounds.

In 1829, Twilight accepted an invitation to head the Orleans County Grammar School in Brownington, Vermont. Thus began one of the most remarkable teaching careers in nineteenth-century America.

The two-story wooden grammar school sat near the top of a broad hill in a thriving village of 400 people. Brownington had been settled by Revolutionary War veterans only thirty years before, and was located on the principal stagecoach route between Montreal and Boston.

Twilight and his wife moved into a small house a few hundred yards from the school and almost immediately began to build a larger house. He found time to serve as minister in the village church, but the school was his passion.

The school, Brownington Academy, was only a few years old, but it enrolled students from every town in the county and was soon over-crowded. Twilight tried to persuade the board of trustees to construct a larger building, but they refused.

So Twilight set about building Athenian Hall, a massive, four-story granite structure that still stands today. In 1834, he laid the foundation for the 36-by-66-foot building. The granite rock for the building was split from two huge boulders found in nearby fields, then shaped with a hammer and chisel. The walls of the school are said to be at least 18 inches thick.

Athenian Hall, which was built across the street from Twilight's home, was completed in 1836. It contained two large classrooms, a

20-by-40-foot assembly hall, six recitation rooms, fourteen student dormitory rooms, a music parlor, a dining room, and a kitchen.

It is not known how Twilight managed to fund the construction, since no public money was used. But the fact that he was able to build Athenian Hall, declared one writer, "way up in the northernmost reach of the state, without financial backing from the county or even much support from within the village itself—testified to the raw power, physical and spiritual, of the man."[1]

Twilight spent most of the rest of his life at the school, overseeing instruction in English, foreign languages, music, and a variety of other courses ranging from philosophy to chemistry. He made sure that students studied the required hours from 9:00 A.M. to 7:00 P.M., and instructed them in the Bible every Sunday evening.

Twilight, America's first black college graduate, helped educate an estimated 3,200 children and grandchildren of the Revolutionary War veterans who settled in Vermont's Northeast Kingdom (the northeastern part of the state). It is not known how many of his students were black, but there were obviously not many. He continued to direct the school until the fall of 1855, when he suffered a stroke that left him paralyzed.

AND THE WINNER IS . . .

Alexander Twilight also made history by becoming one of the first African Americans elected to a state legislature. His fellow town residents sent him, the schoolmaster, to the capital in Montpelier, where he served during the session of 1836–1837, working for better state funding for education. There would not be another black person in the Vermont legislature until 112 years later, when William Anderson was elected in 1948.

Twilight died in June 1857 at the age of sixty-two. His widow survived another twenty-one years. She was buried beside him near his massive stone school. It is not known whether they had any children. The Stone House built by Alexander Lucius Twilight still stands today as a monument to a man of extraordinary courage and perseverance: a man, born when George Washington was president, who gave his life to the education of many of the young nation's earliest students.

PART TWO

✦

THE CIVIL WAR YEARS AND RECONSTRUCTION

S A R A H M A P P S
DOUGLASS

(1806–1882)

Although the vast majority of African Americans continued to be denied even a rudimentary education in the early nineteenth century, a small but growing core of dedicated teachers worked hard to change that.

They were forced to concentrate their efforts in the North, where a tradition of black education was being handed down from generation to generation.

Despite seemingly insurmountable obstacles, some African American families helped educate themselves and others. Sarah Mapps Douglass, who was born in Philadelphia on September 9, 1806, came from such a family.

Her mother's father, Cyrus Bustill, opened a school in his home in Philadelphia shortly after the Revolutionary War and became one of its teachers. He also helped found the Free African Society, which was the first African American benevolent society in the new nation. The motto of the society's members reflected his determination to help other African Americans "to seek out for ourselves."[1] He passed this

belief on to his daughter, Grace. When Grace grew up, she joined with wealthy black shipbuilder James Forten to start a school for black children in Philadelphia.

Grace Bustill married Robert Douglass, who was one of the founders of the First African Presbyterian Church. The Douglass family made sure that their children received an exceptionally good education. Sarah Douglass had tutors for several years, and was then enrolled in her mother's school. Sarah's brother, Robert Jr., went on to attend the Philadelphia Academy of the Fine Arts. Most black children in Philadelphia who tried to obtain an education had to go to private schools run by black men and women. Sarah Douglass, following in her mother's footsteps, opened such a school sometime in the 1820s. It was one of ten black schools in Philadelphia at the time.

Like her forebears, Douglass was active on many other fronts in the fight for racial equality. She was a member of the Philadelphia Female Anti-Slavery Society's board of directors and attended several abolitionist conventions. Her work in the society, which her mother and sixteen other women helped found in 1833 for the purpose of helping escaped slaves, led to friendships with some of the nation's leading white abolitionists.

When Sarah, her mother, and other black guests attended the wedding of white abolitionists Theodore Weld and Angelina Grimké, the Philadelphia press condemned their presence as an intolerable abolitionist incident. Two days later, a mob led by white medical students from the South burned down a shelter for black orphans and the new headquarters of the state anti-slavery society. But Sarah Douglass and her family continued to fight for black equality side-by-side with white people, especially the religious group known as the Quakers.

The Quakers practiced racial discrimination, but they also supported black education. So in 1853, Sarah Douglass accepted a position as head of the girls' primary department in the Quaker-supported Institute for Colored Youth in Philadelphia. This school is now known

It Took Courage to Be a Teacher

In the South, increasingly harsh laws made it illegal to teach free or enslaved black people. These laws were driven by fear, and became even harsher after the uprisings led by Denmark Vesey in 1822 and Nat Turner in 1831. Both men were slaves who had learned to read and write. White southerners were convinced that education had turned these men into dangerous revolutionaries willing to risk their lives to end slavery.

Despite these harsh laws, many African Americans in the South attended clandestine schools or managed to find a brave individual who secretly taught them to read and write.

Even in the North, there was often deep opposition to anyone who believed in educating black people. When future abolitionist and clergyman Henry Highland Garnet and two other black students arrived at the Noyes Academy in Canaan, New Hampshire, in 1834, an infuriated mob tore down the school.

as Cheyney University of Pennsylvania. Cheyney, the oldest black college in the nation, had high scholastic standards but did not teach college-level courses when it began.

Douglass demanded excellence from all her students. In 1864, for example, four of her students at the institute received cash awards for their academic achievements: one for good grades, one for excellence in Latin and Greek, one for excellence in mathematics, and one for good conduct and diligence. Douglass also introduced scientific subjects into the curriculum.

✦ A **curriculum** is the group of courses offered by a school.

In 1855, Sarah married the Reverend William Douglass, rector of St. Thomas Protestant Episcopal Church. He passed away in 1861, at the start of the Civil War. Sarah Douglass remained active in the cause of freedom. She served as vice-chairman of the Women's Pennsylvania

Branch of the American Freedmen's Aid Commission set up at the end of the Civil War.

Most important, she continued to teach at the institute until 1877. Her principal, Fanny Jackson Coppin, was another outstanding African American educator and one of the first black female college graduates in the United States.

Sarah Mapps Douglass passed away in Philadelphia on September 8, 1882. She had spent more than fifty years teaching black youth. Her life was a powerful testament to what a determined person could accomplish even in the segregated society of the mid-1800s.

Many of the young people that she taught, and the generations of students that many of them went on to teach, shared her belief that education could be a powerful force in fighting segregation and racism.

MARY SMITH
PEAKE

(1823–1862)

Mary Smith was born in Norfolk, Virginia, to a white father and a free black mother who were forbidden by law to marry. Young Mary was raised in Alexandria, Virginia, where she lived with an aunt and received a good education. At age sixteen, she returned to Norfolk to live with her mother.

Mary had made up her mind to dedicate her life to helping those less fortunate than herself: the elderly, the poor, and children. Although she had little money, she carried out her work with the help of members of Norfolk's First Baptist Church. She also wanted to teach, and got the opportunity to do so after her mother married Thompson Walker and the family moved to Hampton, Virginia.

There, Mary founded the Daughters of Zion (sometimes called the Daughters of Benevolence) to help the sick and needy. She also began to teach at this time, operating a secret school in her home for children and adults, both enslaved and free.

Although it was still illegal to teach black people to read and write, Mary apparently helped anyone who came to her. The determination

35

of her students to obtain an education must have been as high as Mary's determination to give them one, for many sought her out. During this time, Mary worked as a seamstress to support herself.

In 1851, Mary wedded Thomas D. Peake, who had fought in the Mexican War of 1846–1848. Peake had been born into slavery, but was freed several years before the marriage. The couple had one child, a daughter named Daisy, who was born in 1856.

On the night of August 7, 1861, near the start of the Civil War, Confederate army soldiers burned Hampton. Mary, her husband, and her child were forced to flee across the Hampton River, where they took refuge in Brown Cottage on the grounds of Chesapeake Female College.

Mary's health was failing, but she soon opened a new school—the first of many black schools that would be sponsored by the American Missionary Association (AMA). The school was located on the first floor of Brown Cottage. Mary taught religious and secular lessons to over fifty children there during the day and to twenty adults at night.

The Zion School for Colored Children was one of the many schools started by the Daughters of Zion, the organization founded by Mary Smith Peake to help the sick and needy.

Almost all of her students were escaped slaves who had fled to the Union army at nearby Fortress Monroe when the Civil War began. Located on the Virginia coast, the fortress was in the first area captured by the Union army. Black people called Fortress Monroe "freedom fort" and escaped to it any way they could. Some floated to the fort at night in canoes made of grass. They had twisted grasses to form ropes, which they then bound with other grasses to hold the ropes together. These men, women, and children were eager to learn, and they found in Mary a teacher "who brought to her work manifest excellence along with dedication, and whose school served as an inspired example for those who followed her."[1]

The Reverend Lewis C. Lockwood, the AMA representative who hired Mary, praised her work: "What an impression for good would be made upon the rising generation were this course universally pursued!"[2]

Sadly, Mary Peake died of tuberculosis in February 1862, just five months after starting her school in Brown Cottage. She was the first of hundreds of AMA teachers who dedicated themselves to bringing education to the freedmen, both during and after the Civil War. She set an example the best of them would follow.

Hampton Institute, one of the oldest traditionally black colleges in the nation, was founded by the AMA in 1868 on the grounds where Mary Peake had taught.

ETER HUMPHRIES

CLARK

(1829–1925)

Peter Humphries Clark was born free in Cincinnati, Ohio. That same year, white mobs rioted throughout the city. They burned black homes, stores, and churches, forcing 1,200 black residents to flee to Canada. But Peter's family decided to stay.

Clark's grandfather was said to be the famous explorer William Clark, a slave owner who lived in Virginia. When the Lewis and Clark expedition was commissioned by President Thomas Jefferson in 1803 to explore what is now the northwestern United States, William Clark reportedly moved Peter's slave grandmother and her children to Cincinnati. In doing so, he gave them their freedom.

Peter had little opportunity for education until 1844, when the Reverend Hiram S. Gilmore opened a high school for black children in Cincinnati. Young Peter's eagerness and intelligence were quickly recognized, and he became an assistant teacher while still a student.

The racial prejudice all around Clark disgusted him so much that he considered going to Africa. But he decided to stay in America and fight for his rights. As a youth, Clark had helped fugitive slaves escape

WE WILL PAY OUR TEACHERS!

In 1849, the Ohio legislature passed a law allowing black residents to organize and support their own school with the tax money they paid. Peter Clark was appointed teacher and did his job well, but the Cincinnati city council refused to pay him. The council argued that black people could not employ teachers since they were not recognized as citizens and voters. This argument was overruled in court. Only then could Peter Clark collect his salary.

on the Underground Railroad. Now he began to use his time and talent to help African Americans in other ways. In 1853, he served as secretary of the National Negro Convention in Rochester, New York. The 114 delegates, including Frederick Douglass and most other leading black abolitionists, organized "to command respect for our cause, and to obtain justice for our people."[1] Clark was also active in the National Equal Rights League and established his own newspaper, the short-lived but fiery *Herald of Freedom*. In 1856, Clark helped Frederick Douglass publish *The North Star*, but his most effective efforts in helping his fellow African Americans lay ahead in the field of education.

Clark returned to teaching in the public schools in 1857. His career as an educator would last for the next fifty-one years, thirty of those as the first principal of Cincinnati's Gaines High School for black students. Clark organized an effective school. The demand for his "students as teachers became so urgent that it was for a time difficult to hold them until graduation, so eager were their parents to have them accept jobs."[2]

All sectors of the African American community thought very highly of Clark. The 706 member Black Brigade of Cincinnati, which spent September 1862 strengthening Cincinnati's defenses against a possible Confederate assault, chose Clark to write their official history,

The Black Brigade of Cincinnati, which was published in 1864. He also led the successful fight to establish additional schools for black children in the city, and became Ohio's first black school superintendent.

When racial segregation in the city's public schools was finally abolished in 1887, Clark was removed from the principalship of Gaines High School. During his years at Gaines, Clark had married Frances Williams, an Oberlin College graduate who was a music teacher. The couple had three children, including a daughter who went on to teach school in St. Louis, Missouri. After the loss of his principalship, Clark moved to St. Louis, where he taught at Sumner High School until his retirement in 1908.

Clark's accomplishments as an educator were widely recognized during his lifetime, especially by other African Americans. He served as a trustee at Wilberforce University in Ohio, and received four of fourteen votes for the presidency of Howard University in Washington, D.C., in 1877.

Clark died at his home on June 21, 1925, at the age of ninety-six. His career as an educator and fighter for African American equality had been summed up years before by writer and abolitionist William Wells Brown: Peter Humphries Clark was "an eloquent and splendid speaker possessing rare intellectual gifts, a fine education and [was] one who stood in the foremost rank of the noted men of his race."[3]

PATRICK FRANCIS
HEALY

(1834–1910)

P atrick Francis Healy was this country's first African American Jesuit priest, first African American to earn a doctoral degree in philosophy, and first African American to become president of a Catholic college.

He was born on February 27, 1834, in a log house on a plantation near Macon, Georgia. The plantation was owned by his Irish father, Michael Morris Healy. Patrick's mother was Mary Eliza Smith, a mulatto woman who was owned by Healy. Patrick was one of ten children born to the couple: seven sons and three daughters.

Although Georgia law (like the laws of all southern states and some northern states at the time) considered children born to mothers held in slavery to be slaves themselves, Patrick and his siblings were treated by their father as if they were free.

Like his older brothers, Patrick was sent by his father to a Quaker school in Flushing, New York, for his early education. Upon completion of his studies there, he followed his brothers to Holy Cross

College in Worcester, Massachusetts, where he graduated with a bachelor's degree in 1850.

The education received by the Healy children would have been rare even for white people then, and it was virtually unheard of for black people before emancipation.

A few weeks after graduating from Holy Cross, Patrick entered the Roman Catholic Society of Jesus (Jesuits), and studied with them until 1852. He taught briefly at St. Joseph's College in Philadelphia, and was then transferred to Holy Cross College.

Patrick was described as tall and fair-skinned, with long, flowing hair. His complexion undoubtedly opened doors to him that would have remained closed had he been darker. But he and his brothers sometimes felt the sting of racism.

One of Patrick's younger brothers, Michael, ran away from Holy Cross because of the racial taunts of other students. "Placed in a college as I am, over boys who were well acquainted either by sight or hearing with me and my brothers," Patrick wrote a friend, "remarks are sometimes made . . . which wound my very heart. You know to what I refer. . . . He [Michael] is obliged to go through the same ordeal."[1]

In 1858, Patrick was sent to Europe to continue his studies. He spent most of the next several years studying philosophy and theology in Louvain, Belgium, and was ordained to the Catholic priesthood in 1864. Two years later, he began the career at Georgetown College that would make him famous.

Healy arrived on the campus in Washington, D.C., one year before Congress passed the Thirteenth Amendment abolishing slavery throughout the United States. The young priest started as a professor of philosophy and was appointed dean of the college in 1868. He was so good at leading

✦ A **campus** is the name for the grounds and buildings of a school.

✦ A **university** is made up of more than one college. The courses lead to a bachelor's, a master's, or a doctoral degree.

the other teachers that he was inaugurated as president on July 31, 1874.

During the next eight years, Father Healy improved Georgetown's curriculum. He also established scholarships, improved the libraries, and expanded the college into a university by adding the Georgetown Law School and Medical School.

He dreamed of creating a university that would match the best in Europe. This led him to plan a magnificent seven-story structure on the heights above Georgetown. The constant search for money to fund this project was hard on him, but by 1881 classes were being taught in the first rooms in what quickly became known as the Healy Building. That beautiful structure is still visible today from the Potomac River.

Father Healy's bad health forced him to resign the presidency of Georgetown University in 1882, at the age of forty-eight. He spent many of the remaining years of his life living and traveling with his older brother James.

Patrick Francis Healy passed away in the infirmary at his beloved Georgetown University on January 10, 1910. He was buried almost in the shadow of the Healy Building, part of the great university he helped build in the nation's capital.

THE BROTHERS

Father Healy's brother James was the first African American Catholic bishop in the United States. Bishop James Healy presided for twenty-five years over a diocese in Maine and New Hampshire, where he founded eighteen schools and sixty parishes. He became known as "the children's bishop" for the many orphanages and foundling homes he built, and for his fight against child labor.

Michael Healy, the brother who had run away from Holy Cross College, moved to Alaska. He gained fame as "Hell-Roaring Mike," one of the most colorful Arctic sea captains in history.

CHARLOTTE FORTEN
GRIMKÉ

(1837–1914)

In 1862, the Union army captured the islands off the coast of South Carolina, the home of 10,000 former slaves. Union general William Tecumseh Sherman put out a call for teachers to help educate them. This call was repeated throughout the South. As a result, the Civil War and the years that followed it saw a massive opening up of educational opportunities for black Americans, especially in the South.

During the war, the Freedmen's Bureau opened black schools in areas occupied by the Union army. The bureau was established by the federal government to assist the newly free men, women, and children.

The bureau's greatest success, wrote scholar W. E .B. Du Bois in *The Souls of Black Folk,* "lay in the planting of the free school among Negroes, and the idea of free elementary education among all classes in the South. . . . The opposition to Negro education in the South was at first bitter, and showed itself in ashes, insult, and blood; for the South believed an educated Negro to be a dangerous Negro. And the South was not wholly wrong . . ."[1]

The former slaves joined wholeheartedly in the effort to educate themselves and their children. Many, already laboring long days to support their families, worked extra hours to build schools and pay teachers from the first wages most newly free African Americans had ever received.

Many Northern societies, including the American Missionary Association (AMA), also organized to help start black schools in the South. One of the first Northern teachers to volunteer to teach in the South for the AMA was Charlotte Forten. At the age of twenty-five, she answered her nation's call for teachers.

Born in Philadelphia, Charlotte was the daughter of Robert Bridges Forten and Mary Wood Forten. She was the granddaughter of abolitionist James Forten Sr.

Her father refused to allow her to attend the racially segregated schools of Philadelphia. Instead, he hired private tutors for her early education, and later sent her to the Higginson Grammar School and the Salem Normal School in Salem, Massachusetts.

Charlotte lived in the home of black abolitionist Charles Lenox Remond during her school years in Salem, and became acquainted with anti-slavery leaders William Wells Brown, Lydia Maria Child,

James Forten, grandfather of Charlotte Forten Grimké, was an inventor and successful entrepreneur, who used his wealth to help the poor and needy.

William Lloyd Garrison, Wendell Phillips, and John Greenleaf Whittier.

After graduating from Salem Normal School, she taught at a white grammar school in Salem, but ill health forced her to resign in 1858. She returned to Philadelphia and taught there briefly. Forten also taught one summer in Salem, but continued to be bothered by tuberculosis, then called lung fever.

In spite of her physical problems, Forten eagerly responded when the call went out for teachers in the Port Royal, South Carolina, area. The government had asked for teachers and missionaries to help in a social experiment designed to prove that the former slaves were capable of taking care of themselves.

Forten journeyed south under the sponsorship of the Philadelphia Port Royal Relief Association, one of many groups supported by Northern abolitionist societies. On October 29, 1862, she first saw the school where she was to teach. It was in a small Baptist church on St. Helena's Island, one of many islands around Port Royal.

A CIVIL WAR TEACHER'S DIARY

"We went into the school, and heard the children read and spell," Forten wrote in the journal she kept for many years. "The teachers tell us that they have made great improvement in a very short time, and I noticed with pleasure how bright, how eager to learn many of them seem."[2]

Forten taught youths of all ages in the school, and gave the newly free children the first knowledge of black history they had ever received.

"Talked to the children a little while to-day about the noble Toussaint [L'Ouverture]," she wrote in her diary less than a month after her arrival. "They listened very attentively. It is well that they sh'd know what one of their color c'ld do for his race. I long to inspire them with courage and ambition (of a noble sort), and high purpose . . ."[3]

She also began a night school for the adults after a man named Harry came to one of her classes. She describes Harry in her diary: "He is most eager to learn, and is really a scholar to be proud of. . . . I must inquire if there are not more of the grown people who w'ld like to take lessons at night."[4]

Forten became acquainted with both the officers and the enlisted men of the Fifty-fourth Massachusetts Volunteer Regiment when they were briefly stationed on the island. After their bloody attack on Fort Wagner, she traveled six miles by rowboat from St. Helena's to Beaufort to tend the wounded.

Charlotte Forten's teaching at St. Helena's lasted until May 1864, when she returned to Philadelphia. Her health had worsened again, and she had experienced the sorrow of her father's death. He had become so disenchanted with this country's treatment of black people that he had moved to England. When the Civil War began, however, he quickly returned and enlisted as a private in the Forty-third U.S. Colored Troops. Promoted to sergeant major and assigned to recruit volunteers, Robert Bridges Forten died while on recruiting duty in Maryland and was buried with full military honors.

Charlotte Forten lived quietly for the next several years, winning minor acclaim as a writer. Two of the articles she wrote appeared in the *Atlantic Monthly* and were about her Port Royal experience. She returned to teaching in 1871–1872 as an assistant to the principal of the Sumner School in Washington, D.C., and then went to work as a clerk in the U.S. Treasury Department. In 1878, Forten married the Reverend Francis James Grimké, pastor of Washington's 15th Street Presbyterian Church. The couple had one child, Theodora Cornelia, who died in infancy in 1880.

Charlotte Forten Grimké spent most of the rest of her life in Washington, where she passed away on July 23, 1914.

Her husband, who called her Lottie, said she "was one of the dearest, sweetest, loveliest spirits that ever graced this planet."[5]

The students she taught at St. Helena's would undoubtedly have agreed. She had used education as a tool to help them overcome the ravages of slavery and discrimination, and never lost faith in the ultimate success of their struggle. "The dawn of freedom . . . may not break upon us at once," she wrote at St. Helena's when the Emancipation Proclamation went into effect on New Year's Day 1863, "but it will surely come, and sooner, I believe, than we have ever dared hope before. My soul is glad with an exceeding great gladness."[6]

CARDOZO

(1 8 3 7 – 1 9 0 3)

The southern schools in which teachers such as Charlotte Forten Grimké conducted classes were often old cotton barns, sheds, kitchens, and even tents. Little by little, the terrible conditions improved.

One school was conducted in the mansion of former Virginia governor Henry A. Wise. Wise, who had signed the death warrant for John Brown after the latter's attack on Harpers Ferry, was a Confederate general. His home was captured by Union army soldiers and turned into a school.

By and large, however, one of the most urgent tasks of black men and women throughout the newly liberated areas was providing adequate school buildings and teachers for their children.

During 1867, black men and women built twenty-three schoolhouses in South Carolina, and contributed $12,200 to pay the teachers.

The Freedmen's Bureau, along with northern societies and church groups, also supplied schools and teachers for black children in many southern states. By 1870, there were more than 9,000 teachers and 247,000 pupils in both day and night schools supported by bureau funds.

One of the most successful of the new schools was Avery Institute in Charleston, South Carolina. The school was opened in 1865 with financial support from the American Missionary Association (AMA), the same organization that hired Charlotte Forten Grimké and many of the teachers who came south.

The man who founded Avery and was its first principal was one of the leading black educators and political figures of his day: Francis Louis Cardozo. He would ultimately go down in history for his role in establishing a system of public schools in South Carolina.

Cardozo was born free in Charleston on February 1, 1837, to a Jewish journalist and economist, Jacob N. Cardozo, and a mother who was half black and half Native American.

Determined to receive an advanced education and become an ordained minister, Cardozo worked hard and saved his money to enroll in the University of Glasgow in Scotland. He managed to stay at the university by working as a carpenter during his vacations, and excelling in his studies during the school year.

During a competitive examination with students from the University of Glasgow and three other colleges, Cardozo won a $1,000 scholarship. After four years at Glasgow, he went on to study at Presbyterian seminaries in Edinburgh and London for three more years.

THE CARPENTER'S APPRENTICE

Francis Cardozo attended school only from the ages of five to twelve. Then, like most children of his day, he left school to learn a trade. He worked as a carpenter's apprentice for five years and as a carpenter for four more.

✦ **Apprentices** learn skills by helping experts do their jobs.

Cardozo returned to the United States during the Civil War, and in 1864 was named pastor of the Temple Street Congregational Church in New Haven, Connecticut. He married Catherine Rowena Howell of New Haven that same year, and the couple eventually had four sons and two daughters.

In 1865, Cardozo moved to Charleston to establish Avery Institute and begin his pioneering work in black education in the South. The Avery Institute was located in a building that had housed the state's teacher training school. The property had been offered as a freedmen's school by General Rufus Saxton, assistant commissioner of the Freedmen's Bureau.

Cardozo hired twenty teachers, ten black and ten white. On October 1, 1865, the first day of school, more than 1,000 students greeted them. The building was so crowded that more than 100 students had to be taught in the dome at the top of the building.

Cardozo had organized the school to teach only the earliest grades. Most of the freedmen's schools were organized this way. Many of Avery's students, however, were from Charleston's free black population and already had some education. Cardozo soon initiated more advanced courses for these children, including classics, Latin, and higher mathematics.

One man who visited the school less than two months after it opened said he found "the scholars studious and very orderly, and at all stages of advancement. In a room . . . three hundred children together were taking an object lesson; in another room a class of boys, whose parents, I was told, intended them for professional life, were transposing, analyzing, and parsing a passage from Milton's 'L'Allegro,' and recitations in reading and arithmetic were going on with more or less success before the other teachers."[1]

In 1868, Cardozo was elected as a delegate to the state constitutional convention, which was required under the Reconstruction Acts passed by the federal government. These acts were created to protect

THE BIRTH OF BLACK COLLEGES

Cardozo's introduction of advanced courses at Avery coincided with efforts to establish black colleges in other parts of the South. The North already had three black colleges: the Institute for Colored Youth in Philadelphia, which grew into Cheyney State (1837); Lincoln University in Lincoln, Pennsylvania (1854); and Wilberforce University in Wilberforce, Ohio (1856).

When Avery opened, the AMA also helped organize Atlanta University in Atlanta, Georgia, then followed with the founding of other black colleges: Talladega College in Talladega, Alabama, in 1867; Hampton Institute (to train black farmers) in Hampton, Virginia, in 1868; and Tougaloo College in Tougaloo, Mississippi, in 1869.

Fisk University, which the AMA helped found in Nashville, Tennessee, in 1867, was originally housed in old army barracks. Spelling books and Bibles were bought with money raised from the sale of iron handcuffs and chains from the slave pens in Nashville. In the first year of its existence, 1,000 students enrolled.

the rights of black citizens. He was appointed to the position of chairman of the committee on education, and it was in this role that Cardozo helped plan a system of public schools for South Carolina, which his fellow delegates voted to approve.

"It is sufficient to say . . . that for the first time the fundamental law of the state carried the obligation of universal education and demanded the creation of a school system like that of Northern states,"[2] wrote one man about the delegates' approval of Cardozo's plan.

That same year, and again in 1870, Cardozo was elected as South Carolina's secretary of state. He was the first black person in the United States elected to a state cabinet office. Cardozo was appointed professor of Latin at Howard University in 1871, but soon returned to South Carolina, where he was elected state treasurer in 1872 and 1874. The end of Reconstruction in 1877 and the return of white domination, and the oppression that followed, led to the end of his political career.

Returning to Washington, he helped educate many more black students while serving as principal of the Colored Preparatory High School from 1884 to 1891, and of the M Street High School from 1891 to 1896.

Francis Louis Cardozo died in Washington on July 22, 1903, after decades of working to improve the education of African American children. In 1928, a business high school was named in his honor in the nation's capital. His greatest legacy, however, was the public school system he helped establish in South Carolina and the countless children of all races he helped educate.

JAMES MILTON
TURNER

(1840–1915)

J ames Milton Turner was born into slavery on May 16, 1840, in St. Louis County, Missouri, the son of John and Hannah Turner. His father, having previously bought his own freedom, managed to buy both James and his mother out of slavery when the child was four years old.

James learned to read in a secret school for black children conducted by nuns in the St. Louis Catholic Cathedral. When the school was discovered and closed by police, he started attending another secret school held by the Reverend John Berry Meachum in the basement of the First Baptist Church in St. Louis. James and his parents were determined that he be educated. Despite the risks, they even obtained lessons for him "from a white religious zealot who defied the laws of the state [that forbade the education of black people] because he believed all persons should be able to read the Bible."[1]

When James was fourteen, his parents helped him enroll in the preparatory department of Oberlin College in Oberlin, Ohio. He was an eager student. Unfortunately, when his father died, he had to

return home to support his mother. His school days were suddenly over, but no one could take his education away from him. His love for learning survived. During his long life, he would help found Lincoln University in Jefferson City, Missouri, and serve as a U.S. diplomat to Africa.

The Civil War began when Turner was twenty-one. Assigned as a valet to a Union officer, Turner was wounded in the hip at the Battle of Shiloh. The Emancipation Proclamation of 1863 had still not been issued when he returned home, so he started helping fugitive slaves trying to escape to the North. "Often, at night," said a friend, "he tied a skiff containing a fugitive slave to the stern of a steamboat and was towed to the Illinois shore."[2] James Turner was a courageous young man whom others respected.

After the North won the war, the first tax-supported school for black children in Missouri was established. Turner was appointed to teach in the school located in Kansas City. A few months later, he took charge of the black schools in Booneville, Missouri. People could see that he was a leader.

AN ENTERPRISING EDUCATOR AND GENEROUS SOLDIERS

Turner longed to establish a school to train more teachers. He discussed the idea with many of the black Union army soldiers he met during the war.

In 1866, he used his contacts with the soldiers and got them to donate approximately $5,000 to make his dream a reality. This amazing sum, along with money contributed by members of the Sixty-second and Sixty-fifth U.S. Colored Troops, helped build Lincoln Institute (renamed Lincoln University in 1921) in Jefferson City, Missouri. The soldiers' money bought a plot of land and paid for the institute's first small school building.

As a result of Reconstruction, black people could vote and partic-ipate in politics for the first time. Turner used this new power to advance the cause of black education.

In 1870, he presided over a convention to advance the education of black people in Missouri. Under Turner's leadership, the convention "presented to the Legislature the draft of a bill to endow Lincoln Institute as a State Normal School for training colored teachers."[3] The legislature approved the bill, and pledged $15,000 annually to support the school.

The legislature also appointed Turner assistant state superinten-dent of schools with the responsibility of establishing Negro schools. There are no records detailing Turner's actions as superintendent, but he is said to have worked closely with the Freedmen's Bureau.

Turner became the leading black politician in Missouri during Reconstruction, and was a strong supporter of President Ulysses S. Grant. This support was rewarded in 1871, when Grant appointed him minister resident and consul general to Liberia. He was the sec-ond African American to enter the U.S. diplomatic corps. The first was Ebenezer Bassett, who was appointed minister to Haiti and the Dominican Republic in 1869.

Turner spent seven years in Liberia, and returned home in tri-umph in 1878 after being honored at several receptions in Europe. One of the receptions was in England at Windsor Castle, where his host was the Prince of Wales, later King Edward VII.

Turner married Ella de Burton of St. Joseph's Parish, Louisiana, shortly after returning home. The couple never had children.

He continued to work for black Americans for the rest of his life. When the Cherokee nation received money from Congress for lands taken from them at the end of the Civil War, the Cherokees refused to share any of the money with the black people who had lived among them. Blacks ran into the same problem with the Delaware, Shawnee, Choctaw, and Chickasaw nations. Turner successfully argued their

EXCELLENCE IS REWARDED

George B. Vashon, a black educator, attorney, and writer who was a friend of Turner's, described the joy with which Turner's successful career was greeted by black Americans:

"Boston, New York, Philadelphia and Washington vied with each other in the splendor of the banquets with which they welcomed the homecoming of the black man whose public service they recognized as a vindication of the emancipation proclamation and the Fifteenth Amendment [which gave African Americans the right to vote]."[4]

Vashon said that in St. Louis, "the horses were taken from the carriage in which Turner rode from the railway station and exuberant Negroes dragged the momentary idol through the streets."[5]

claims and helped an estimated 3,500 black people share in the congressional payments and land distributions to those nations.

Turner was fatally injured in Ardmore, Oklahoma, in 1915 when a railroad tank car exploded and partially wrecked the home where he was staying. He died a month later, on November 1, 1915. His wife had passed away seven years before.

James Milton Turner helped bring education to uncounted numbers of African American youth. An editorial writer in a St. Louis newspaper described him as a person whose life had been "possessed of inextinguishable hope, deep passion and purpose to which was added a national scope of activity."[6]

The man who had traveled so far from home, was buried just ten miles from the plantation where he was born.

SUSIE KING
TAYLOR

(1848–1912)

Of all the black men and women teachers during the Civil War, Susie King Taylor was probably the one most directly involved with teaching black Union army soldiers.

Born into slavery on the Isle of Wight off the coast of Georgia, about 35 miles from Savannah, Susie was the first of nine children born to Raymond Baker and Hagar Ann Reed.

When Susie was seven, her owners allowed her and one of her brothers to travel to Savannah to live with their grandmother. The grandmother was a strong-willed woman determined to do whatever she could to help her family survive. Realizing the value of education in the fight to end slavery, she defied laws that made it a crime for black people to learn to read and write, and sent the children to a secret school run by a free African American woman.

Police strictly enforced laws prohibiting the education of black people, and Susie and her brother faced the danger of harsh whippings if they were caught.

"We went every day about nine o'clock, with our books wrapped in paper to prevent the police or white persons from seeing them," she remembered decades later. "We went in, one at a time, through the gate, into . . . the L kitchen, which was the schoolroom." At the end of the school day, said Susie, "we left the same way we entered, one by one, when we would go to a square . . . and wait for each other."[1]

Neighbors sometimes saw the children, but assumed they were learning a trade. It was legal throughout the South for black people to learn to work with their hands, but not for them to learn to use their minds.

Susie attended this school for about two years, then continued studying with another woman. She also received instruction from the white landlord's son and daughter, who were also her playmates.

Every black person, both free and enslaved, had to have a pass to be on the streets after the curfew bell rang at 9:00 each night. Susie used her knowledge to write passes for her grandmother and other black adults, allowing them to move freely after the curfew.

In April 1862, Susie was sent back to her mother. Union army soldiers were firing on nearby Fort Pulaski on the Georgia coast, and she

A TEENAGER STARTS A SCHOOL

Susie and her family ended up on St. Simon's Island at the beginning of the Civil War. Just a few days after arriving, the fourteen-year-old was asked by a navy officer if she would start a school.

She eagerly agreed, "and in a week or two I received two large boxes of books and testaments from the North. I had about forty children to teach, besides a number of adults who came to me nights, all of them so eager to learn to read, to read above anything else."[2]

experienced the Civil War for the first time. "I remember what a roar and din the guns made," she said. "They jarred the earth for miles."[3]

Susie soon married Edward King, a sergeant in Company E of the newly formed First South Carolina Volunteers (later renamed the Thirty-third U.S. Colored Troops). The regiment was the first in the Union army composed entirely of former slaves, and several of these soldiers were Susie's uncles and cousins.

She was employed as the regiment's laundress, but also served as nurse and teacher. "I taught a great many of the comrades in Company E to read and write, when they were off duty," she said. "Nearly all were anxious to learn. My husband taught some also when it was convenient for him. . . . I gave my services willingly for four years and three months without receiving a dollar."[4] The soldiers' eagerness to learn was typical of black soldiers throughout the army.

BLACK SOLDIERS EVEN CARRIED THEIR BOOKS INTO BATTLE

Almost every black regiment established a school whenever it was not on the move or fighting, even though the school was often nothing more than a group of men seated around a campfire with their spelling books.

"Their ambition to learn to read and write was as strong as their love of freedom," wrote one colonel about the men in the black regiments, "and no opportunity was lost by them to acquire a knowledge of letters. So ardent were they that they formed squads and hired teachers, paying them out of their pittance of seven dollars per month, or out of the bounty paid to them by the State to which they were accredited."[5]

Black soldiers even carried their books into battle, and when the belongings of those who were killed were collected, their comrades "often found in the dead soldier's knapsack a spelling book and a Testament."[6]

Susie King and her husband returned to Savannah after the war was over. There was no public school in the city for black children, so she opened a school in her home. "I had twenty children at my school, and received one dollar a month for each pupil," she said. "I also had a few older ones who came at night."[7]

In 1866, Edward King died. Susie King gave birth to a baby boy shortly afterward and tried to support herself and her son with the income from the school. She was forced to close the school, however, when a free school was opened nearby. During the next few years she opened two more schools, but was forced to close each one when free schools took away her pupils.

Susie King went to work as a laundress for a wealthy white couple in 1872, and traveled north with them two years later. She spent most of the remaining years of her life in Boston, where she married Russell L. Taylor in 1879.

She spent the rest of her life trying to keep the accomplishments of the black Union army soldiers from being forgotten, and speaking out against the anti-black violence that swept the South following the end of Reconstruction.

In 1893, she was elected president of the Boston branch of the Women's Relief Corps, the auxiliary to the Grand Army of the Republic (GAR). The GAR was an organization of Union army veterans dedicated to keeping alive the memory of their fallen comrades, and to fighting for pension increases and other benefits for veterans.

She returned to the South in 1898 to visit her dying son in Shreveport, Louisiana. Because of racism, she was unable to obtain a berth on the train to take him back with her to Boston. Since that was the only way he could travel in his condition, she was forced to leave him in Shreveport, where he died soon afterward.

Susie Taylor published her memoirs in 1902 and passed away in 1912. Her life had been one of service to other African Americans, especially during the Civil War and the years immediately following.

"I have received letters from some of the comrades, since we parted in 1866," she wrote more than thirty years later, "with expressions of gratitude and thanks to me for teaching them their first letters."[8] Her ability to give them the gift of knowledge seemed to mean as much to her as it meant to them, and that is probably how Susie King Taylor most wanted to be remembered: as a teacher for her comrades.

PART THREE

✦

INTO THE NEW CENTURY

Booker T.
WASHINGTON

(1856–1915)

✦

During Reconstruction, African Americans gained the right to be educated and the right to vote. But swiftly, through violence, fraud, and legal tricks, black people in the South lost virtually all the rights they had gained. Public schools that had been opened to them were closed. Without the right to vote, there was little they could do about it. Once again, the question arose: Who would teach the poor and the newly free people?

One of the great educators who tried to figure out a way was Booker Taliaferro Washington. He was born into slavery on April 5, 1856, in Franklin County, Virginia. His mother, Jane, was enslaved, and his father was a white man he never knew.

When he was nine years old, he was sent to work in a salt mine by his stepfather, a man named Washington Ferguson whom his mother married sometime after Booker was born. Between the ages of ten and twelve, Booker also worked in coal mines near his home in Malden, Virginia, as did many other children at the time. The work was hard and dangerous.

Eager to learn, Booker managed to obtain a little schooling before and after work. His mother also arranged for the teacher from the local black school to give him lessons at night. As he recalled years later, "[we were] a whole race trying to go to school. Few were too young, and none too old, to make the attempt to learn. As fast as any kind of teachers could be secured, not only were day-schools filled, but night-schools as well."[1]

One day while working in the coal mine, he heard two miners talking about "a great school for coloured people somewhere in Virginia. . . . As they went on describing the school, it seemed to me that it must be the greatest place on earth."[2] The school was the Hampton Normal and Agricultural Institute (later Hampton Institute). In 1872, the eager sixteen-year-old began the 500-mile journey to the school, walking most of the way. He arrived with fifty cents in his pocket.

His decision to enroll in Hampton was probably the most important one of his life. The school's principal was General Samuel Chapman Armstrong, a man who had commanded black Union army soldiers in the Civil War. He quickly befriended Washington and arranged for a white northern philanthropist to pay the young man's tuition. Washington paid for his room and board by working as a janitor at the school.

- ✦ A **philanthropist** is someone who gives money to various needy causes for humanitarian reasons.
- ✦ When you pay for your education, you are paying **tuition.**
- ✦ You receive **vocational** education or training when you learn a skill or trade.

Washington said he received two great benefits from his years as a student at Hampton: the friendship of Armstrong and the knowledge of the importance of vocational education: "labour, not alone for its financial value, but for labour's own sake and for the independence and self-reliance which the ability to do something which the world wants done brings."[3]

Washington graduated from Hampton in 1875 and returned home to Malden to teach. In 1879, he went back to Hampton to teach in a program for Native Americans, where he remained for two years.

In 1881, through the influence of General Armstrong, Washington was offered a position that would bring him worldwide fame: the principalship of a high school to train black teachers in Tuskegee, Alabama. The school had been authorized by the Alabama legislature and the twenty-five-year-old Washington quickly accepted the offer. But when he arrived, he found that the legislature's $2,000 appropriation covered only salaries. There were no school buildings or land.

He recruited students from throughout the county, and held the institute's first classes in a shanty near the black Methodist church. The church was used as an assembly hall. Washington said the shanty was in such poor shape "that, whenever it rained, one of the older students would very kindly leave his lessons to hold an umbrella over me . . ."[4]

All of Tuskegee's buildings were constructed by the students, with Washington determined that they "would be taught to see not only

THE PRINCIPAL BUILDS HIS SCHOOL

A personal loan from the treasurer at Hampton Institute enabled Booker T. Washington to buy an abandoned plantation on the edge of Tuskegee, Alabama. The mansion on the plantation had been burned down, but he had the Tuskegee students repair a stable and a henhouse for use as classrooms. Black residents in the area contributed whatever money they could toward buying materials for a new building. One farmer who had no money, gave a "fine hog."

A white sawmill owner supplied the lumber, even though Washington could not pay him until much later. With this help, and money from several whites in the North, Washington put the thirty students to work erecting Tuskegee's first new building.

Tuskegee students gather for a history class in one of the many classrooms built with the skillful hands of students.

utility in labour, but beauty and dignity . . ."[5] By 1888, Tuskegee owned 540 acres of land, had an enrollment of over 400, and offered courses in printing, cabinetmaking, carpentry, farming, cooking, sewing, and other vocational skills. In 1896, the young scientist George Washington Carver joined the faculty as director of agricultural research. Washington believed in practical, vocational education. Not only did it give people skills to make a living, but also gave them independence and self-reliance.

Washington was not the first black educator to teach the virtues of self-reliance, though none did it more successfully. His name became a household word throughout the country, however, for another reason. In his "Atlanta Compromise" speech on September 18, 1895, at the opening of the Cotton States and International Exposition in Atlanta, Georgia, Washington urged black Americans to accept segregation and its second-class status.

The legendary educator Booker T. Washington poses with a group of Tuskegee Institute teachers and trustees.

He declared: "The wisest among my race understand that the agitation of questions of social equality is the extremest folly . . ."[6]

Black members of the audience wept openly at this surrender of their dreams of equality, but the majority of white Americans loved the speech. White editorial writers and politicians took it upon themselves to proclaim Washington the new black leader (Frederick Douglass, the leading African American for decades, had died a few months before).

John D. Rockefeller, Andrew Carnegie, and other wealthy industrialists contributed money to Washington for black education. Presidents Theodore Roosevelt and William Howard Taft consulted him on which black Americans should receive governmental jobs. But Washington's critics charged that his opposition to nonvocational academic training for black people would keep black people on the bottom rungs of society's ladder.

Washington was a more complex man than some of his critics realized. Though he told black people to accept segregation, he also fought behind the scenes to end it. His work encouraging an investigation into black peonage (semi-slavery) in Alabama helped bring about a federal judge's declaring the practice unconstitutional.

In 1904, Washington secretly financed a legal challenge against

Alabama for denying qualified black people the right to vote. He financed successful appeals in an Alabama case involving the exclusion of black people from a jury. He also helped challenge transportation laws requiring separate seating for blacks and whites. These actions were done so carefully that few black people, and almost no white people, knew about them.

In the latter years of his life, Washington was helped at the institute by its principal—his third wife, Margaret Murray Washington. They were married in 1893. Washington's first wife, Fannie M. Smith, had died in 1884 after two years of marriage. They had one daughter. In 1885, Washington had married a second time to Olivia A. Davidson, the assistant principal of Tuskegee. She died in 1889, leaving him two sons.

Washington passed away at Tuskegee from heart disease and overwork on November 14, 1915, at the age of fifty-nine. His funeral, which was held three days later in the Tuskegee Institute Chapel, was attended by almost 8,000 people. A special train bearing dignitaries came from New York City.

Booker Taliaferro Washington was buried in a brick tomb on a hilltop that overlooked the institute. Fittingly enough, the tomb was built by his students with bricks that they made.

WHO IS RIGHT, BOOKER T. OR W. E. B.?

The black scholar and leader W. E. B. Du Bois summed up his opinion of Washington and the passive path he urged blacks to follow in his famous "Atlanta Compromise" speech in *The Souls of Black Folk:* "So far as Mr. Washington preaches Thrift, Patience, and Industrial Training for the masses, we must hold up his hands and strive with him. . . . But so far as Mr. Washington apologizes for injustice . . . and opposes the higher training and ambition of our brightest minds,—so far as he, the South, or the Nation, does this,—we must unceasingly and firmly oppose them."[7]

MARY CHURCH

TERRELL

(1863–1954)

Mary Church Terrell was born in Memphis, Tennessee, on September 23, 1863, to Robert R. Church Sr. and Louise Ayers Church, both born into slavery. After the Civil War, Robert Church became one of the richest black men in America. He was a real estate dealer and founder of the Solvent Savings Bank and Trust Company in Memphis.

Determined that Mary would receive a better education than the segregated schools of Memphis could provide, her parents sent her to the Antioch College Model School in Yellow Springs, Ohio, when she was about six years old. Though so light-skinned that she was often mistaken for white, Mary was sometimes the butt of racist deeds and words. As a result of these incidents, she resolved to show that she was academically superior to the white students, and went on to finish first in her class.

In 1879, Mary enrolled in Oberlin College in Oberlin, Ohio, and set out to study the four-year "gentleman's course" rather than the two-year curriculum usually assigned to female students.

She graduated from Oberlin in 1884, and became one of the few black women in the country who had ever earned a bachelor's degree. Though she was eager to share her knowledge with young black students, her father wanted her to return home rather than go to work. She reluctantly complied—for a few months.

Soon, bored with simply acting as a hostess to the many guests in the home of her millionaire father, she accepted a position as an instructor at Wilberforce College in 1885.

Her father was furious at her decision and "disinherited me, refused to write to me for a year. . . . Further I was ridiculed and told that no man would want to marry a woman who studied mathematics. I said I'd take a chance and run the risk."[1]

Mary taught at Wilberforce for two years, then moved to Washington, D.C., to teach Latin in the Preparatory School for Colored Youth (renamed the M Street High School in 1891). There she worked under the direction of Robert Heberton Terrell, whom she married in 1891. At the time, married women were legally barred from working as teachers in Washington, so Mary Terrell again spent her time running a household.

The year after her marriage, however, an event occurred that turned her into the outspoken activist she would remain for the rest of her life: Her friend Tom Moss was lynched in Memphis.

Terrell began organizing black women for the struggle against racism and sexism. She became president of the Colored Women's League, which merged in 1896 with the Federation of Afro-American Women to form the National Association of Colored Women (NACW). Terrell was chosen president of the NACW, a group she would be associated with for the rest of her life.

In 1895, she was appointed to the District of Columbia School Board, the first black woman to hold the position. Terrell served eleven years on the board, always fighting for equal treatment for African American students and faculty members. During those years, she was also struggling in her personal life. Terrell suffered three miscarriages, which she blamed on inferior hospitals for black people in

Washington. In 1898, she traveled to New York to be with her mother and gave birth to a daughter she named Phyllis (in honor of the black poet Phillis Wheatley). She and her husband later adopted one of her nieces, Roberta Church. But Terrell never paused in her crusade for justice.

THE MAKING OF A CRUSADER

Mary Terrell and Tom Moss had been friends since childhood. He was a guest at her wedding and the owner of People's Grocery in Memphis.

Many whites in Memphis had long been furious that Moss's grocery store took business from a white-owned store in the black community. Moss's store was also a gathering place for black people. One Saturday night in 1892, a white mob attacked the store. It was full of black men, many of them armed. They repelled the mob, wounding three of them. Moss, his two co-owners, and 100 other black men were arrested. The white press called them "brutes" and "criminals" who had attacked "innocent" whites.

In the predawn hours of March 9, 1892, Moss and his two friends were taken from their cells and lynched. The mob then looted and destroyed People's Grocery.

There had been 255 lynchings in 1892, but these struck Mary Terrell personally. "Lynching can never be suppressed in the South, until the masses of ignorant white people in that section are educated and lifted to a higher moral plane . . . ," she declared. "Lynching cannot be suppressed in the South, until all classes of white people, . . . learn a holy reverence for the law."[2] She and Frederick Douglass met with President Benjamin Harrison and urged him to publicly condemn racist violence. He listened politely but refused to speak out.

From that time on, Mary Terrell fought against injustice with all her might.

She attended the founding conference of the National Association for the Advancement of Colored People (NAACP) in 1909. The conference had been called by W. E. B. Du Bois and other black leaders determined to wage a vigorous fight for equal rights.

She marched with white feminists, but chided them for their indifference to black concerns.

Terrell's husband passed away in 1925. Grieving over his loss and disillusioned by the suffering of black Americans during the Great Depression and the years that followed, Terrell became increasingly militant as she grew older.

In 1946, she began a three-year battle to gain membership in the all-white Washington chapter of the American Association of University Women. Her efforts were successful when the anti-black members of the chapter resigned, and the remaining members of the chapter invited Terrell to join them.

The biggest victory during the latter part of her life came in her challenge to segregation in Washington's public accommodations. In 1949, she was elected chairman of the newly organized Coordinating Committee for the Enforcement of the District of Columbia Anti-Discrimination Laws, which had been passed during Reconstruction but never enforced.

On February 28, 1950, at the age of eighty-six, she led two other black women and one white woman into the segregated Thompson Restaurant in Washington. Employees refused to serve the black women, and they challenged the refusal in court.

For the next three years, leaning on a cane for support, she helped lead boycotts, sit-ins, and picketing of department stores with restaurants that refused to serve African Americans. Her efforts ended in victory in 1953 when the U.S. Supreme Court ruled that segregated eating facilities in Washington were unconstitutional.

In spite of her age, Terrell was still not finished with her struggle against injustice. When Georgia officials sentenced black sharecropper

Rosa Ingram and her two sons to death for killing a white man who attacked her, Terrell agreed to head the National Committee to Free the Ingram Family.

She spoke at the United Nations, and traveled to Georgia in an unsuccessful attempt to win a pardon from the governor. The Ingrams were finally freed in 1959, five years after Terrell's death.

Fittingly, just two months before Terrell's death, the Supreme Court outlawed public school segregation in its *Brown* v. *Board of Education of Topeka* decision. Terrell's life work of teaching and fighting injustice, from the time her friend was lynched almost sixty-two years before, had done much to prepare the downfall of legal segregation in the nation's schools and elsewhere.

Mary Church Terrell passed away on July 24, 1954, at the age of ninety.

She once wrote proudly that she was a "meddler" determined to "investigate institutions, customs, and laws whose effect upon the citizens of any color or class is depressing or bad."[3]

Today, her memory is honored by a school in Washington, D.C., named after her, as well as many black women's clubs.

ROBERT RUSSA
MOTON

(1867–1940)

Robert Russa Moton, successor to Booker T. Washington, as principal of Tuskegee Institute, was born in Amelia County, Virginia, on August 26, 1867.

According to family legend, Moton's great-great-great-grandfather had been a powerful African chief. Robert's parents, Booker and Emily Brown Moton, worked on a plantation and had little money. But they did everything in their power to educate their son. Robert's mother gave him his first lessons in reading, and the plantation owner later arranged for one of his daughters to teach him. When a former Confederate officer opened a school for black children, Robert was able to attend the third grade.

Although he loved schooling, his studies always had to take a backseat to whatever work he could find to help the family. He was therefore rarely able to attend school for more than a few weeks at a time while he was a child, and he once worked in a lumber camp for two years.

Determined to be educated, Robert journeyed to Hampton Institute in Virginia in 1885 and took the entrance examination. His earlier training was so poor that he failed. But he was given a job in the school sawmill and allowed to attend school at night. Within a year, he had caught up enough to attend regular day classes.

Robert graduated from Hampton in 1889, and remained at the school as drillmaster and assistant commandant in charge of the semi-military student body. The next year, he was promoted to commandant with the title of "major," a position he held for the next twenty-five years. His leadership brought him widespread recognition in a variety of fields.

Robert Moton admired Booker T. Washington and shared many of his ideas. Like Washington, Moton believed that African Americans needed to work hard, avoid confronting white Americans with demands for racial equality, and have faith that a conciliatory attitude would one day result in racial progress.

In 1900, Moton was elected president of the National Negro Business League, which had been formed by Washington to promote black businesses throughout the nation. Within five years, the league had grown to more than 100 chapters.

In 1905, Moton married Elizabeth Hunt Farris, who passed away a few months later. In 1908, he married a fellow Hampton graduate and teacher, Jennie Dee Booth. The couple had five children: three girls and two boys.

Moton frequently traveled with Washington to promote their shared ideas of vocational education and racial conciliation. The two also attended joint fundraising meetings with northern philanthropists, who were Hampton's and Tuskegee's most powerful supporters. When Washington died in 1915, Moton was appointed to take his place.

Like his predecessor, Moton became an adviser to U.S. presidents on race relations and federal appointments. He served in that capacity with Presidents Woodrow Wilson, Warren G. Harding, Calvin Coolidge, and Franklin D. Roosevelt.

In 1918, two weeks after the signing of the armistice that ended World War I, Wilson sent Moton to France to investigate charges of racism and mistreatment of black American soldiers. Many white Americans feared the soldiers would cause trouble when they returned home by demanding to be treated with equality because of their battlefield valor. Army officials, having similar fears, spread rumors that the soldiers had behaved badly and should be closely watched when they came back home.

Many African Americans feared that Moton would urge the soldiers not to insist on their rights, especially after he told the soldiers not to protest against the racism they were experiencing from white American officers and soldiers.

WINNING THE FIGHT FOR BLACK CONTROL

Moton became more assertive at home in the years following the war. He compiled statistics on the lynching of black Americans and saw that they were widely publicized. He even persuaded the government to build a black veterans' hospital on land donated by Tuskegee Institute.

White officials tried to control the hospital, which opened in 1923. They demanded white doctors and nurses, with black people hired only as menial workers. "You understand," a prominent white citizen told him in 1923, "that we have the legislature, we make the laws, we have the judges, the sheriffs, the jails. We have the hardware stores and the arms."[1]

Moton's fight for black control of the hospital brought pressure and threats from white residents and members of the Ku Klux Klan. He refused to back down, however, and the hospital was staffed completely by African American doctors, nurses, and other employees.

"He and the Negro world demanded that the government hospital at Tuskegee be under Negro control," wrote W. E. B. Du Bois in 1924. "Today, at last, it is."[2]

In one speech, he told the black soldiers to go home "in a straight-forward, manly and modest way,"[3] implying that they should not expect to enjoy democracy at home because they had fought for it abroad. But Moton also surprised his critics by condemning racism in speeches to white officers and soldiers. The recommendations he made improved some of the conditions the black soldiers labored under, and brought about the dismissal of a white general widely viewed as anti-black.

Returning to Tuskegee, Moton saw the need for better-trained black teachers and workers in all fields. He opened a "college department" in the 1925/26 school year. Black students at Tuskegee were now able to study the college-level subjects that Washington had often ridiculed, with bachelor of science degrees being offered in education and agriculture.

Dr. George Washington Carver, scientist and inventor, did groundbreaking research at the Tuskegee Institute and invented many useful products in the field of agriculture. In his laboratory at Tuskegee, he helped many students discover the exciting world of science.

Moton's most lasting legacy to Tuskegee, however, was his successful campaign to increase the school's endowment and expand its facilities. When he took over in 1915, the school's

endowment was slightly more than $2.3 million. By the time he retired twenty years later, the endowment was almost $8 million.

Moton served on many private and government bodies during his career, including the Commission on Interracial Cooperation in 1918 (which he persuaded George Eastman of the Kodak Corporation to fund); the Hoover Commission on the Mississippi River Flood Disaster in 1927; the U.S. Commission on Education in Haiti in 1930 (which he headed); and as president of the National Business League.

Moton received several honorary degrees during his career at Tuskegee, including a Master of Arts from Harvard University, and Doctor of Letters degrees from Howard University, Virginia Union University, Wilberforce University, Oberlin College, and Williams College. He also received the Harmon Award for Distinguished Achievement in Education in 1930, and the NAACP's Spingarn Medal in 1932 for distinguished service to African Americans.

Moton retired from Tuskegee in 1935 because of ill health, and spent the last years of his life at his home in Capahosic, Virginia, enjoying his favorite pastime: fishing in the York River. He died on May 31, 1940, and was buried at Hampton Institute.

His almost fifty years as an educator were controversial among African Americans, with criticism for his failure to speak out and act against racial injustice, and praise for the advances he made at Tuskegee.

Robert Russa Moton moved in a racially hostile world and made compromises some other black leaders refused to make. But he also accomplished much for Tuskegee Institute and the people it served.

JOHN
HOPE

(1868–1936)

J ohn Hope, the first black president of Atlanta University, was born on June 2, 1868, in Augusta, Georgia. His mother was Mary Fanny Frances, a black woman, and his father was James Hope, a native of Scotland who had made a fortune as a planter.

The interracial couple lived together in a wealthy home and often played host to some of the best-known white citizens in Augusta. When John Hope's father died in 1876, the executors of the estate robbed young Hope's mother of all but a tiny part of her inheritance. At that moment, Hope said decades later, he became aware that he was "only another colored boy."[1]

Though almost penniless, young John was bright. After completing the eighth year of schooling in Augusta's public schools in 1881, he was given scholarships to Worcester Academy in Worcester, Massachusetts. There, he excelled in both academics and athletics, though he had to work part-time to meet expenses. He graduated with honors in 1890.

He then won a scholarship to Brown University in Providence,

Rhode Island, where he also excelled, despite working in a restaurant several days a week. Hope was chosen as class orator at his graduation from Brown in 1894, with a Bachelor of Arts degree.

After graduating from Brown, Hope joined the faculty of Roger Williams University in Nashville, Tennessee, from 1894 to 1898, teaching Latin, Greek, and the natural sciences.

He was present when Booker T. Washington made his famous "Atlanta Compromise" speech in 1895, and reacted angrily to Washington's acceptance of segregation and inequality. "If we are not striving for equality," Hope asked in an 1896 speech before a black Nashville debating society, "in heaven's name for what are we living?"[2] That same year, he also publicly demanded that African

A FAIR CHANCE TO LEARN IS A WEAPON

John Hope was light-skinned enough to pass for white, but always insisted on being recognized as black. His experience as a boy in the South helped him see clearly the connection between education and economic equality.

Booker T. Washington had promised white America that he would support only education that "would make the Negro humble, simple, and of service to the community." But John Hope saw education as a weapon in the larger struggle to achieve equality. Black students needed a fair chance to learn, and Hope knew they were not getting it.

In the South during the 1880s and 1890s, states spent only a fraction of the money on black students that they spent on white students.

In 1915, there were only a handful of black elementary schools in each southern state. Most of these were one-room shacks that were open only three or four months a year.

In 1916, North Carolina had only nineteen black high school students in the state, and there were only sixty-seven black public high schools in the entire South. As late as 1920, 85 percent of all black students in the South were confined to the first four grades, with no further education available to them.

Americans should have the same educational opportunities as white Americans.

"The Negro must enter the higher fields of learning," he said. "He must be prepared for advanced and original investigation. . . . Mere honesty, mere wealth will not give us rank among the other peoples of the civilized world; and . . . we ourselves will never be possessed of conscious self-respect, until we can point to men in our own ranks who are easily the equal of any race."[3]

During Christmas vacation in 1896, Hope married Lugenia Burns of Chicago. She would bear him two sons and work closely with him throughout his career. She was also involved in many of her own social causes, including being one of the first volunteer social workers in Atlanta.

In 1906, Hope became the first black president of Atlanta Baptist College (renamed Morehouse College in 1913). There he put his beliefs about higher education into practice. Morehouse became known as the "college of presidents" because of its many graduates who became presidents of black colleges. Two of them were Mordecai W. Johnson, president of Howard University, and John W. Davis, president of Virginia Collegiate Institute (later called West Virginia State College).

One of Hope's best friends was W. E. B. Du Bois. When Du Bois and other leaders organized the Niagara Movement in 1905 (the forerunner to the NAACP), Hope was the only black college president who dared defy Booker T. Washington and his white supporters by attending.

He was also the only college president, black or white, who joined the protest meetings in 1909 that led to the founding of the NAACP. His greatest educational achievement, however, was in creating a new Atlanta University. The new university unified several competing black colleges in Atlanta into one system that was stronger and much more efficient than any of the single institutions. The new Atlanta University was made up of Morehouse College, Spelman College, the

WHAT DOES A COLLEGE PRESIDENT DO?

As a college president, John Hope set high standards. First, he changed the Morehouse curriculum. Then he increased the college enrollment and gained financial support from northern philanthropists. This support came about after his longtime friend, Robert Russa Moton, convinced Booker T. Washington to help on Hope's behalf.

From 1920 to 1929, Hope helped build what was called the "Greater Morehouse." Using contributions from African Americans, as well as large donations from the General Education Board and the American Baptist Home Mission, Hope presided over the construction of several new buildings and an enrollment that quickly tripled.

original Atlanta University, Morris Brown College, Clark College, and Gammon Theological Seminary.

Hope was elected president of the new Atlanta University in 1929. In cooperation with Morehouse and Spelman, the university began offering graduate-level courses.

In the years to come, Hope's dream of a university as good as any school in the United States became a reality. He hired some of the best teachers in the country, including Du Bois, and they taught a wide range of subjects. He established graduate schools of liberal arts and social work, a school of business administration, a library school, and a department of music and fine arts. Eventually, the university added the master's and doctorate degrees, the first from any black institution.

Between 1931 and 1936, ninety-three students earned their master's degrees at Atlanta University. In addition, many public school teachers were able to do advanced study in their fields during the summer sessions.

Hope received many awards during his lifetime, including election to Phi Beta Kappa (Brown University) as an Alumni Member in 1919, the Harmon Award for Distinguished Achievement in Education among African Americans in 1929, and an honorary LL.D. degree from Brown in 1935.

John Hope passed away on February 20, 1936. His services were held in the Morehouse Chapel, and students carried his body to a simple grave near the site of his old office.

Many years before, Hope had expressed the belief that African Americans had within them "emotional, spiritual elements that presage gifts . . . more ennobling and enduring than factories and railroads and banks."[4]

That belief in the gifts of his fellow African Americans led John Hope to build "an edifice at which the Negro can obtain higher education comparable to that obtainable in any other part of the country," declared the president of the General Education Fund at Hope's funeral.

"His accomplishments entitle him to a foremost place among educational statesmen."[5]

W. E. B.
DU BOIS

(1868–1963)

Villiam Edward Burghardt (W. E. B.) Du Bois, one of the greatest scholars the world has ever known, and founder of the modern African American civil rights movement, was born on February 23, 1868, in Great Barrington, Massachusetts.

His father, Alfred Du Bois, died before Will was old enough to remember him. His mother, Mary Silvina Du Bois, had to struggle to make ends meet for herself and her son.

When she passed away in 1884, young Du Bois went to work in a local mill. He continued to excel at Great Barrington High School, where he was the only black student. He graduated the same year his mother died. A few months later, the principal helped arrange a church scholarship for him to attend Fisk University in Nashville, Tennessee.

Du Bois arrived at Fisk in the fall of 1885, and he never forgot his first day there: "It was to me an extraordinary experience," he wrote. "I was thrilled to be for the first time among so many people of my own color or rather of such various and such extraordinary colors . . ."[1]

During summer vacations, he taught black students in rural Tennessee. After three years at Fisk, he had gained a lot of insight into the depths and complexities of racism.

Du Bois graduated with a bachelor's degree from Fisk in 1888, and entered Harvard University as a junior. There he graduated cum laude with a Bachelor of Arts in 1890 and earned a Master of Arts degree in history in 1891.

He studied at the University of Berlin in Germany for two years after graduating from Harvard. Europe was the first place he had ever lived without race prejudice, and this had a profound effect upon him. "I ceased to hate or suspect people simply because they belonged to one race or color," he said.[2]

The next few years, Du Bois began an academic career that brought him nationwide attention. From 1895 to 1897, he taught English, Latin, Greek, and German at Wilberforce University. There he met and married Nina Gomer in 1896. The couple had two children: Burghardt Gomer, who died while still a baby, and Nina Yolande.

When his son died, Du Bois sat down and wrote what many have called the most searing essay in the history of race relations: "On the Passing of the First Born." It included this passage: "All that day and all that night there sat an awful gladness in my heart . . . and my soul whispers ever to me, saying, . . . 'not dead, but escaped, not bond, but free.' No bitter meanness now shall sicken his baby heart till it die a living death."[3]

In 1899, Du Bois's book *The Philadelphia Negro*, a survey he conducted of the social, racial, and economic conditions of black Philadelphians, was published. The book was the first in-depth study of an urban African American community. Today, it is still considered a significant work of its kind.

From 1897 to 1910, Du Bois taught history and economics at the old Atlanta University. During that time, he published fourteen studies on African Americans that were so important he could later say

What Are Your Plans for the Future?

One night in 1893, alone in his small room in Berlin, Du Bois realized what he wanted to do with his life. "These are my plans," he wrote, "to make a name in science, to make a name in literature and thus to raise my race."[4]

Du Bois quickly made a name for himself. He received a Ph.D. degree in history from Harvard in 1895. He was the first African American to receive a doctorate from Harvard. His Ph.D. dissertation, *The Suppression of the African Slave Trade to the United States of America, 1638–1870*, was the first of nineteen books (both nonfiction and fiction) he would write.

truthfully: "Between 1896 and 1920 there was no study in America which did not depend in some degree upon the investigations made at Atlanta University . . ."[5]

He had enjoyed friendly relations with Booker T. Washington for several years. In 1903, however, with the publication of *The Souls of Black Folk,* Du Bois posed a direct challenge to Washington's philosophy of compromising black equality.

In a period when the South averaged five lynchings of African Americans a day, when black southerners in rural areas were being reduced to a condition of semi-slavery, and when Black Codes forced thousands of innocent black men, women, and children to work as unpaid labor on chain gangs and plantations, Du Bois declared: "We have no right to sit silently by while the inevitable seeds are sown for a harvest of disaster to our children, black and white."

Instead, he urged black Americans to unite with white Americans who believed in racial equality, and to use "force of every sort: moral persuasion, propaganda and . . . even physical resistance."[6]

Rather than concentrate on vocational training, he urged higher academic training for what he called the Talented Tenth (the top 10 percent) of black students, who could then go on to help teach, inspire, and lead the masses. He also practiced what he preached. In 1905, Du Bois was one of the founders of the Niagara Movement, a group of black professionals and intellectuals whose aims were to fight for full equality in every area of American life.

Booker T. Washington used his influence to try and destroy the new organization, but he failed. In 1909, the Niagara Movement merged with the National Association for the Advancement of Colored People (NAACP). Du Bois served as an officer in the new group.

In 1910, he left Atlanta University to join the NAACP in New York City as its director of publications and founder and editor of its magazine *The Crisis*.

In the pages of *The Crisis*, Du Bois supported American involvement in World War I. But after the war, the widespread lynchings and raw racism inflicted on African Americans led him to declare that all "of us fools fought a long, cruel, bloody, and unnecessary war, and we not only killed our boys—we killed Faith and Hope."[7]

While serving as the editor in chief of The Crisis *magazine, W. E. B. Du Bois started a new magazine just for children called* The Brownies' Book. *It was an entertaining and educational magazine, and children from all over the country could send in their stories, poetry, and letters.*

In 1919, he began trying to unite people of color throughout the world by organizing the First Pan-African Congress in Paris. In the years to come, he organized several more congresses in Paris, Brussels, and London in 1921; in Lisbon and London in 1923; and in New York City in 1927. Although delegates attended from many parts of the world, the idea of Pan-Africanism did not develop a strong following until decades later.

The Great Depression of 1929–1941 led Du Bois to conclude that the NAACP needed to change drastically. In his view, racism existed because it was profitable to white Americans to exploit black Americans. Du Bois said that what was needed to fight racism was black economic power, even if it meant temporarily accepting racial segregation.

NAACP officials, who were committed to working for integration, were horrified at his ideas. In June of 1934, they forced him to submit his resignation. Du Bois was now sixty-six years old, but he was about to embark on some of the most productive years of his life.

He returned to Atlanta University, where he taught for another ten years and produced two of his finest books: *Black Reconstruction in America: An Essay Toward a History of the Part Which Black Folk Played*

THE POWER OF THE PEN

For twenty-four years, through the power of his pen, Du Bois turned *The Crisis* into one of the most powerful publications the United States has ever known.

His NAACP colleagues would later say that the ideas Du Bois expressed in *The Crisis* "and in his books and essays transformed the Negro world as well as a large portion of the liberal white world. . . . He created, what never existed before, a Negro intelligentsia. . . ."[8]

✦ A group of very smart people is sometimes called an **intelligentsia.**

in the Attempt to Reconstruct Democracy in America, 1860–1880 (1935), and *Dusk of Dawn: An Essay Toward an Autobiography of a Race Concept* (1940). In 1944, he returned to the NAACP as director of special research. There he served as an associate counsel to the American delegation at the founding of the United Nations in 1945, speaking out strongly for independence for European colonies in Africa and Asia.

Du Bois also helped revive the Pan-African movement. He attended the Fifth Pan-African Congress in Manchester, England, in 1945, and presided over several sessions. Delegates from sixty countries and colonies elected him permanent chairman and president, and he was widely recognized as "the father" of Pan-Africanism.

In 1961, he and his second wife, Shirley Graham Du Bois, moved to Accra in newly independent Ghana, at the invitation of its first president, Kwame Nkrumah. Du Bois's first wife had died in 1950. He became a citizen of Ghana and settled down to work on a long-dreamed-of project: the *Encyclopedia Africana.*

On August 27, 1963, Du Bois passed away at the age of ninety-five. The government of Ghana honored him with a state funeral, and he was buried in Accra.

Word of his death came to a small meeting of African Americans in Washington, D.C., on the eve of the March for Jobs and Freedom, where the Reverend Dr. Martin Luther King Jr. made his famous "I Have a Dream" speech. Author John O. Killens said someone told those at the meeting that "the old man" had died, and everyone knew without asking that "the old man" was Du Bois. For generations of African Americans, he was also, as Killens described him, "our patron saint, our teacher and our major prophet."[9]

His tremendous contributions to scholarship and the cause of human freedom were recognized by honorary degrees from Howard, Atlanta, Fisk, and Wilberforce Universities and several foreign universities.

MARY McLEOD
BETHUNE

(1875–1955)

Mary McLeod Bethune, adviser to U. S. presidents and founder of Bethune-Cookman College in Daytona Beach, Florida, was the seventeenth child born to Samuel and Patsy McLeod, both former slaves. Mary was the first of their children born free.

Her parents owned five acres they had bought from her mother's former master in Mayesville, South Carolina, where they grew rice and cotton. They also owned the cabin they lived in, having cut the trees and built the home with their own hands. On the day of Mary's birth, July 10, 1875, her mother "exulted, 'Thank God, Mary came under our own vine and fig tree.'"[1]

Young Mary became fired with the determination to learn when a white girl snatched a book from her hands. Black people could not read, the girl told her, and so the book was not meant for her. But despite Mary's desire to learn, "it was almost impossible for a Negro child, especially in the South, to get an education," she wrote more than fifty years later. "There were hundreds of square miles,

104

I Want to Read!

"Every morning I picked up a little pail of milk and bread, and walked five miles to school," Mary McLeod Bethune recalled, "[and] every afternoon, five miles home. But I walked always on winged feet."[2]

A new world opened up for her when she learned to read, especially verses from the Bible that told of God's love for all people. "With these words the scales fell from my eyes and the light came flooding in," she said. "My sense of inferiority, my fear of handicaps, dropped away."[3]

sometimes entire states, without a single Negro school. . . . Mr. Lincoln had told our race we were free, but mentally we were still enslaved."[4]

All that changed for Mary when a young black woman was sent by the Missionary Board of the Presbyterian Church to open a school for black children. With the support of her parents, Mary enrolled in the school.

When she had to stop going to school in order to help out on the farm, she said: "I used to kneel in the cotton fields and pray that the door of opportunity should be opened to me once more, so that I might give to others whatever I might attain."[5] With the help of scholarships from a Quaker woman in Colorado, Mary McLeod attended and graduated from Scotia Seminary in Concord, North Carolina, and Moody Bible Institute in Chicago, Illinois.

At age twenty, she began teaching at the Haines Normal and Industrial Institute in Augusta, Georgia, working closely with the school's founder, Lucy Laney. The school offered courses for black students from the elementary grades through high school. Laney, a black woman, convinced Mary McLeod that one of the greatest needs of African Americans was for dedicated teachers like herself.

McLeod next taught in Sumter, South Carolina, where she met and married Albertus Bethune in 1897. The couple had a son, and Mary stopped teaching "so that I could be all mother for one precious year. After that I got restless again to be back at my beloved work . . ." Her husband passed away soon afterward, and in 1904, Mary McLeod Bethune moved to Daytona Beach with the dream of opening a school for black children.

She had only $1.50, but rented a shabby, four-room cottage by promising to pay $11 a month. She began making the rounds of black churches, where ministers allowed her to speak and take contributions.

On October 3, 1904, Bethune opened her school "with an enrollment of five little girls, aged from eight to twelve, whose parents paid me fifty cents' weekly tuition. My own child was the only boy in the school. Though I hadn't a penny left . . . I had faith in a living God, faith in myself, and a desire to serve."[6]

The next year, the school was chartered as the Daytona Normal and Industrial Institute for Negro Scholars. Lacking money to buy supplies, Bethune and the students burned logs, then used the splinters as pens. They obtained "ink" by mashing elderberries.

Within two years, the school had grown to several teachers, many volunteers, and 250 students. Bethune rented a large hall next to the cottage, using it as a combination classroom and dormitory for the students who boarded. She made mattresses out of corn sacks, and filled them with Spanish moss she picked from trees. At this time, Bethune began to concentrate more on the education of girls because they had fewer opportunities than boys.

Desperately needing room for a larger campus, she approached the owner of a local dump called "Hell's Hole." He agreed to sell her the land for $250, with $5 down. Bethune did not even have $5, but promised to return with it in a few days. She raised the money by selling ice cream and sweet-potato pies to black construction workers, and took the money to the owner wrapped in her small handkerchief. "That's how the Bethune-Cookman college campus started," she said.[7]

She wanted to construct a new building on the site, but again had no money. Mary Bethune pleaded with contractors for loads of free sand and used bricks, and promised workmen free sandwiches and free tuition for themselves and their children in exchange for a few hours' work in the evenings. In 1907, the building they erected was opened on the new campus, and Mary Bethune called it Faith Hall.

The black people of Daytona Beach and surrounding communities also gave all they could, even if it was just a nickel or a dime. Mary Bethune was a strong believer in interracial cooperation, and invited white visitors to attend Sunday services at the college. As a result, every Sunday some of the largest interracial crowds in the South worshiped on Mary Bethune's campus.

THE WEALTHY VISITOR

Mary McLeod Bethune scanned the local newspapers for names of prominent visitors from the North, and wrote letters inviting them to visit her. One of those who responded was James N. Gamble, owner of Procter & Gamble Enterprises. He arrived at the campus one day and was shocked by its shabby appearance and lack of buildings.

"Where is the school?" he asked.[8]

"It is in my mind and in my soul," Mary Bethune replied.[9]

Gamble gave her a check and agreed to become the school's first trustee. Other wealthy people also helped, including Thomas H. White, owner of the White Sewing Machine Company. The trust fund White left enabled the school to build White Hall, its main assembly hall, in 1918.

✦ A **trustee** takes responsibility for supervising and caring for something.

✦ A **trust fund** is property or money that is held in safekeeping for the future.

As the school expanded, Bethune said, "whenever I saw a need for some training or service we did not supply, I schemed to add it to our curriculum. Sometimes that took years."[10]

One day, one of her students became critically ill with appendicitis, but there was not a single hospital in Florida that would accept black patients. Bethune begged a white doctor to operate on the young woman, and he finally agreed. A few days later, however, when she visited the student, she "found my little girl segregated in a corner of the porch behind the kitchen. Even my toes clenched with rage."[11]

Within days, she had persuaded three friends to buy a small cottage behind Faith Hall, where she opened a two-bed hospital. It quickly grew to twenty beds, staffed by both black and white physicians and student nurses from the college. The McLeod Hospital served both students and African Americans throughout the state for twenty years, until Daytona Beach finally agreed to provide medical care for black people.

In 1922, the college merged with Cookman College for black men, to form Bethune-Cookman College. There were now fourteen modern buildings on a 32-acre campus with an enrollment of 600. Mary Bethune's work was supported by several black leaders, including Mary Church Terrell of the National Association of Negro Women and Booker T. Washington.

Her accomplishments as an educator opened many doors, and she used them to help African Americans throughout the nation. She was an adviser to Presidents Calvin Coolidge and Herbert Hoover. President Franklin D. Roosevelt invited her to the White House in 1934, and chose her to serve on the Advisory Committee of the National Youth Administration (NYA).

The next year, she was appointed director of the NYA's Division of Negro Affairs, making her one of the few African Americans with direct access to the president. Among her accomplishments as director were the securing of funds for Bethune-Cookman and other black colleges.

Always a strong believer in the power of coalitions to bring about change, Mary Bethune organized the National Council of Negro Women (NCNW) in 1935, which united several black women's associations.

She also helped found the "Black Cabinet" in 1936. The cabinet, made up of African Americans holding positions in the Roosevelt administration, lobbied for African Americans to be included in the programs of Roosevelt's New Deal.

In 1936, she was elected president of the Association for the Study of Negro Life and History, which had been founded by Dr. Carter G. Woodson and several other black men in 1915.

Bethune had received many honorary degrees and other awards in the decades since her "childish visions in the cotton fields," including the Spingarn Medal from the NAACP (1935), the Frances Drexel Award for Distinguished Service (1937), the Thomas Jefferson Award for outstanding leadership (1942), the Medal of Honor and Merit from the Republic of Haiti (1949), and the Star of Africa from the Republic of Liberia (1952).

In the Last Will and Testament that she wrote for black Americans, she said: "I leave you love; I leave you hope; I leave you a thirst for education. . . . I leave you a desire to live harmoniously with your fellow men; I leave you a responsibility to our young people."[12] Mary McLeod Bethune died in her Daytona Beach home on May 18, 1955, at the age of seventy-nine. Her funeral services were held in the Bethune-Cookman Auditorium and she was buried on the campus she loved so much.

Carter G.
WOODSON

(1875–1950)

Carter Godwin Woodson, widely praised as the founder of Negro History Week (later changed to Black History Month), was born on December 19, 1875, in New Canton, Virginia, to James and Anne Eliza Woodson. He was the oldest of nine children. His parents were so poor that all the children had to work to help the family survive.

Like Booker T. Washington, young Carter spent much of his youth working in the local coal mines. As a result, he was largely self-taught until he was seventeen. In 1892, Carter and his family moved to Huntington, Virginia, where he had hoped to attend all-black Douglass High School. But he had to work in the coal mines again, and could not attend school full-time until 1895, when he was twenty years old.

Carter completed high school in a year and a half, and soon afterward was admitted to Berea College in Berea, Kentucky. Berea was one of the few predominantly white colleges in the country that admitted black students, especially poor ones who had to work their way through school. Working as a school principal to support himself, Woodson maintained an average grade of 91 percent at Berea and

CARTER G. WOODSON
TEACHER, HISTORIAN, PUBLISHER

FROM 1903 TO 1906, DR. WOODSON WAS A SUPERVISOR OF SCHOOLS IN THE PHILIPPINES. HIS HEADQUARTERS WERE LOCATED NEAR THE SPOT WHERE THE FIRST JAPANESE FORCES LANDED AFTER PEARL HARBOR.

BORN OF EX-SLAVE PARENTS, YOUNG WOODSON COULD ONLY ATTEND SCHOOL ON RAINY DAYS, WHEN WORK ON THE FARM WAS IMPOSSIBLE. AT 17, HE WAS A MINER IN WEST VIRGINIA!

DR. WOODSON, THROUGH HIS SCHOLARLY WRITINGS, IS RESPONSIBLE, MORE THAN ANY OTHER SINGLE PERSON FOR FAMILIARIZING THE AMERICAN PUBLIC WITH THE CONTRIBUTION OF THE NEGRO TO WORLD HISTORY. HE IS THE ORIGINATOR OF NEGRO HISTORY WEEK, AND FOUNDER OF THE ASSOCIATION FOR THE STUDY OF NEGRO LIFE AND HISTORY. HIS WORKS ON NEGRO HISTORY ARE TO BE FOUND IN THE LIBRARIES OF EVERY IMPORTANT INSTITUTION OF LEARNING.

Alston for OWI

graduated with a bachelor of letters degree in 1903. The year after Carter graduated, Kentucky passed a law prohibiting black students from attending Berea College.

Nothing could keep Carter Woodson from learning. From 1903 to 1906, he served as supervisor of schools in the Philippine Islands, which the United States had annexed after winning the Spanish-American War. He learned to speak Spanish fluently and took courses at the University of Chicago by correspondence while in the islands.

He then spent a year traveling and studying in North Africa, Asia and Europe, including a semester at the University of Paris, where he became fluent in French. On returning to the United States, Woodson received a Bachelor of Arts degree from the University of Chicago on March 17, 1908, and a Master of Arts degree on August 28, 1908.

Woodson's enthusiasm for knowledge only grew greater with each passing year. After a year of further study in history and political science at the Harvard School of Arts and Sciences, he moved to Washington, D.C. There he began the work in black history that made him famous—research at the Library of Congress for his doctoral dissertation, "The Disruption of Virginia." It earned him a Ph.D. in history from Harvard University in 1912.

From 1909 to 1918, Woodson taught at the M Street and Dunbar High Schools. In 1918–1919, he served as principal of Armstrong High School and was on the faculty of Miner Normal School in Washington, D.C.

It was a time of great turmoil for African Americans throughout the nation. In the nation's capital there were widespread efforts to make black Americans permanent second-class citizens. Woodson, like W. E. B. Du Bois and many other black educators, believed that ignorance of black history and accomplishments fueled much of this anti-black feeling.

Du Bois fought the ignorance with his writings in the NAACP's magazine, *The Crisis*. Woodson, however, saw the need for a new organization. On September 9, 1915, he and several other black men met in

Chicago and founded the Association for the Study of Negro Life and History (ASNLH). The word *Negro* was later changed to *Afro-American*. The purpose of the ASNLH was to promote historical research about black people, find and preserve their historical records, publish books on African American history, and promote that history through schools, colleges, clubs, churches, and fraternal organizations.

In 1916, Woodson began editing the ASNLH's journal, *The Journal of Negro History.* In 1925, he organized the Associated Publishers, to publish books about African Americans that white publishers would not print.

For several years, Woodson had combined teaching with his other activities, serving as dean of Howard University's School of Liberal Arts and head of the Graduate Faculty in 1919 and 1920, and dean of the West Virginia Collegiate Institute (later West Virginia State College) in 1920–1922.

In 1922, however, he decided to retire from teaching to devote the rest of his life to writing about, editing, and popularizing black history. That same year, he published his book *The Negro in Our History,* which became the most widely used black history book in high schools, colleges, and universities for more than a decade.

Woodson would eventually write and edit more books on African American history than anyone before him. Some of his scholarly works are *The Education of the Negro Prior to 1861* (1915); *The Negro Wage-Earner* (1930), with Lorenzo Greene; and *The Mis-Education of the Negro* (1933). He started the *Negro History Bulletin* in 1937.

Among the books Woodson wrote for young people are *Negro Makers of History* (1928), for junior high school students; and *The Story of the Negro Retold* (1935), for high school students.

He was honored for his achievements with the NAACP's Spingarn Medal in 1926 and a Doctor of Laws degree from Virginia State University in 1941.

Carter Godwin Woodson died of a heart attack in his Washington home on April 3, 1950. He had never married. His life's work, declared African American historian John Hope Franklin, had been a "valiant attempt to force America to keep faith with herself, to remind her that truth is more praiseworthy than power, and that justice and equality, long the stated policy of this nation, should apply to all citizens and even to the writing of history."[1]

THE FATHER OF BLACK HISTORY MONTH

In order to reach larger numbers of people than those who read his journal, Woodson began Negro History Week in 1926. He knew that celebrating black history was important. "The hidden truths revealed at last to such large numbers," he wrote years later, "exposed the bias in textbooks, bared the prejudice of teachers, and compelled here and there an enrichment of the curricula by treating the Negro in history as we do the Hebrew, the Greek, the Latin, and the Teuton."[2]

Even in the midst of the Great Depression, he successfully appealed to African Americans for help in keeping Negro History Week alive. Thus were planted the seeds for Black History Month.

MORDECAI WYATT
JOHNSON

(1890–1976)

Mordecai W. Johnson, noted Baptist minister and the first black president of Howard University, was born in Paris, Tennessee, on January 12, 1890. The son of the Reverend Wyatt Johnson (a Baptist minister) and Carolyn Freeman Johnson, he attended the lower grades in the Paris public school.

Because there was no high school for black students in the town, his mother sent him to the Baptist high school at Roger Williams University in Nashville, Tennessee, paying his way with money she earned from sewing. When the high school burned down, she sent him to another Baptist school, Howe Institute, in Memphis. Mordecai graduated from Howe when he was sixteen and entered the Atlanta Baptist College in 1906.

"There," he said, "I was thrown at once under three of the greatest teachers I have ever known: Samuel Archer, Benjamin Brawley, and John Hope."[1]

Mordecai was an outstanding athlete in college, as well as an accomplished singer, but he loved public speaking most of all and was

captain of the debating team. In the years to come, he became known throughout the nation as a gifted, though sometimes long-winded, speaker. "The Lord told me to speak," he often told audiences, "but He did not tell me when to stop."[2]

Johnson graduated from Atlanta Baptist in 1911. He taught history, English, and economics there until 1913, when the school received a new charter and was renamed Morehouse College.

His mother, whom he had been especially close to, died while he was teaching at Morehouse. After the funeral, he sat in a chair all night trying to figure out what to do with the rest of his life. "Before that night was over," he declared, "I knew that I had found the meaning of life—service to the poor and needy, service to my race. And I felt that the way to give that service was by entering the ministry."[3]

He received an A.B. degree from the University of Chicago in 1913, then continued his studies at the Rochester Theological Seminary in Rochester, New York, receiving a Bachelor of Divinity degree from the school in 1921. He graduated from Harvard University the following year with a Master of Theology degree, and gained national recognition for the address he gave as one of the commencement speakers.

In a speech titled "The Faith of the Negro," delivered at a time of widespread anti-black violence and oppression, Johnson said African Americans "have come to the place where their faith can no longer feed on the stones of repression and violence. They ask for the bread of liberty, of public equality, and public responsibility. It must not be denied them."[4]

Johnson had been ordained a Baptist minister in 1916. That same year, he married Anna Ethelyn Gardner, and the couple eventually had three sons and two daughters. Johnson served as pastor of the First Baptist Church in Charleston, West Virginia, for nine years, and became a driving force in the community. He organized a branch of the NAACP, established a cooperative grocery store for African Americans, and made his church the center of community life.

He loved pastoring, and planned to do it for the rest of his life. In 1926, however, he was offered an opportunity to influence both the spiritual and the intellectual life of African Americans throughout the country as the president of Howard University. Johnson accepted, and on September 1, 1926, he was sworn in as the first black president of the university that had been founded in 1867.

When Johnson took over, Howard University consisted of a cluster of departments rather than colleges, and none of the departments were accredited. Only half of the faculty members taught at the school full-time. The majority of the school's funding came from the U.S. Congress, and was subject to the whims and prejudices of the congressmen.

Johnson quickly set about reorganizing the university. He hired more full-time faculty members, built a better relationship with Congress, and began seeking more money from private sources. From 1930 to 1940, every school in the university was reorganized and approved by national associations. A strong believer in the brotherhood of all people, regardless of race, religion, or nationality, Johnson expanded the faculty to include "Negroes and whites, men and women, Protestants, Catholics, Jews, Free-Thinkers and atheists,

Howard University, one of America's historically black universities, is shown here in 1870, three years after it opened its doors to students, and fifty-six years before Mordecai Johnson was sworn in as its first black president.

The Champion of Free Speech

According to Howard history professor Rayford W. Logan, "Faculty members could say and write and teach whatever they wanted to, within reason, because President Johnson was one of the most fearless critics of American democracy in modern times."[5]

In 1958, the Washington, D.C., commander of the Veterans of Foreign Wars (VFW) tried to stop a lecture at Howard being given by W. E. B. Du Bois, because of the black scholar's criticisms of U.S. policies. Johnson not only made sure the lecture was held, but sat in the front row and was one of the first to congratulate Du Bois when he finished speaking.

Americans, Europeans, Latin Americans, Asians, and Africans. We even have a few Republicans," he said.[6]

Johnson spent thirty-four years as Howard's president. During his tenure, the university constructed twenty new buildings, including research libraries and laboratories. Johnson also saw to it that more than half of the new faculty members he hired held doctorate degrees.

Among the outstanding black scientists and scholars he brought onto the faculty were Ralph Bunche, Everett Just, Charles R. Drew, E. Franklin Frazier, Kenneth B. Clarke, William L. Hansberry, Rayford W. Logan, and Alain Locke.

The law school and the medical school became universally respected for their excellence, and a 1965 survey showed that over half the black doctors then practicing in the United States were graduates of Howard.

Johnson retired as president on June 30, 1960, and was designated president emeritus of the university. President-elect John F. Kennedy sent a message to Johnson that said, "You have truly been one of the outstanding leaders in American education in this century."[7]

Johnson retired to his home in Washington, where he and his wife often played host to their friends and children. As the years went by, they were blessed with twenty grandchildren and six great-grandchildren. Mrs. Johnson died in 1969, and Johnson married Anna Ethelyn Gardner.

On September 11, 1976, Mordecai Wyatt Johnson passed away at his home. He was eighty-six years old. He had received many honors during his lifetime, including the NAACP's Spingarn Medal in 1929, nine honorary degrees from colleges and universities, and awards from the governments of Ethiopia, Haiti, Liberia, and Panama. In 1973, Howard University had named an administration building after him.

Another pastor who became a force in education is William H. Gray III, president of the United Negro College Fund. Gray is a passionate and active supporter of the forty-one historically black colleges and universities in the United States.

INTO THE FUTURE—HISTORICALLY BLACK COLLEGES AND UNIVERSITIES TODAY

William H. Gray III is president of the United Negro College Fund (UNCF) and a former congressman. Gray has used all his skills as a minister and a politician to help the UNCF and the almost 60,000 students enrolled in Historically Black Colleges and Universities (HBCUs).

There are forty-one HBCUs, and all except one (Wilberforce University in Wilberforce, Ohio) are in the South. Over 90 percent of the students in the HBCUs require financial assistance.

As the Executive Officer of the UNCF, Gray quickly challenged leaders in government and industry to support educational systems throughout the nation with more than words. "It's as if people believe we can have major educational change without committing any major resources," he said. "There's tremendous frustration building up."[8]

During the first two years he headed the UNCF, it raised almost $200 million. More than 60 percent of the students the UNCF helped "are the first members of their family to attend college," Gray said. "Fifty percent come from homes with family incomes below $25,000. Ten percent of all black Ph.Ds attend Morehouse. Forty percent of all black pharmacists attend Xavier."[9]

Every year, hundreds of African Americans graduate from the HBCUs with degrees in math and science. A third of all black students who receive bachelor's degrees earn them at HBCUs, and more than 40 percent of the black students who earn doctorate degrees did their undergraduate work at historically black institutions.

Gray says the work of the UNCF is at least as important now as it was when it was first proposed in 1943 by Dr. Frederick Patterson, president of Tuskegee Institute. Distinguished alumni include the Reverend Dr. Martin Luther King Jr., opera singer Leontyne

> ✦ **Alumni** are people who have graduated from a particular school, college, or university. A male graduate is called an **alumnus.** A female graduate is an **alumna.**

Price, poet Nikki Giovanni, civil rights leader and politician Andrew Young, former surgeon general of the United States Dr. Joycelyn Elders, and filmmaker Spike Lee.

WILLIAM LEO
HANSBERRY

(1894–1965)

William Leo Hansberry dedicated a lifetime to destroying the myth that Africans were savage, ignorant people who had never contributed anything to civilization. The pioneering historian who spent more than forty years uncovering the history of ancient and medieval Africa was born in Gloster, Mississippi, on February 25, 1894, to Eldon Hayes Hansberry and Harriet Pauline Hansberry. His father, a history professor at Alcorn A & M College, died when Hansberry was almost three. But the large library he left contained many books on history, which the young boy read while growing up.

The books told him much about ancient Greece and Rome. As he grew older, however, he realized he had "exceedingly limited knowledge of Black Africa's story in olden days."[1]

He enrolled in Atlanta University in 1914, and one day came across a book that was to influence the rest of his life: *The Negro* by W. E. B. Du Bois. The book's chapters on African civilizations were the first Hansberry had ever seen describing such achievements. He

123

eagerly searched out other books Du Bois had cited in his "Suggestions for Further Reading" section.

"I was profoundly moved by what Du Bois had to say . . . ," he remembered. "I discovered, however, that most of these references were not available in the Atlanta University library or elsewhere in the city. It was then I decided to go to Harvard . . ."[2]

+ **Archaeology** is the scientific study of past human life and activities.

+ **Sociology** is the scientific study of society and its institutions.

+ **Psychology** is the scientific study of the human mind and behavior.

Hansberry transferred to Harvard College, where he plunged into the study of African archaeology and anthropology. He managed to work his way through school as a bellhop and a janitor, but there were times when he had to go hungry.

While still enrolled at Harvard, he taught history, African archaeology, sociology, and psychology at Straight College in New Orleans for one year. He received his Bachelor of Science from Harvard in 1921, and spent the summer visiting black schools and colleges "in an attempt to bring to the attention of teachers and students the significance of ancient African civilization."[3]

He began teaching at Howard University in 1922 as Special and Part-time Lecturer on Ancient African Civilizations.

His courses were the first of their kind to be given at any American university. He offered them along with additional African history courses at Howard for the next thirty-seven years. By 1924, his classes held 800 eager students, many of them Africans who had never been taught their own heritage.

Hansberry taught that mankind's origins were in Africa. Now that is a generally accepted view, but in 1924 he was labeled a lunatic. Two Howard professors urged the president to fire him because he "was endangering the standards and reputation of the university by teaching matters for which there is no foundation in fact."[4]

The president and the board of trustees voted to end Hansberry's

LOOK IT UP!

With the help of the Library of Congress, the Howard University library, some friendly colleagues, and his own money, Hansberry was able to do original research and write about his discoveries about Africa.

He reminded students that the "idea that civilizations originated in tropical Africa is clearly expressed in a number of early Greek historical writings and this idea prevailed throughout the Middle Ages and in early modern times."[5]

His knowledge of civilizations was vast. Ethiopia was a center of trade and government more than 1,000 years before Christ. Ghana (A.D. 800–1000) and Songhai (A.D. 1400–1700) were deliberately "buried in the morgue of history," Hansberry declared.

Hansberry pointed out that "centuries before the geographical and historical terms Babylon, Assyria, Persia, Carthage, and Etruria, or for that matter Greece and Rome themselves, had made their first appearance in the writings of classical authors, Ethiopia was already an old and familiar expression . . ."[6]

program, but later rescinded that decision. Hansberry, who never publicly expressed anger at his detractors, said his colleagues had made their charges as a result of their own ignorance of African history.

Hansberry continued to expand his knowledge throughout his career, receiving an M.A. degree in anthropology from Harvard in 1931. He could not study for a doctorate in African studies because no American college or university offered such a degree at that time.

Hansberry also did postgraduate research at the University of Chicago's Oriental Institute from 1936 to 1937, and at Oxford University's School of Anthropology and Archaeology from 1937 to 1938.

In 1938, he married Myrtle Kelso Hansberry. The couple had two daughters, Gail Adelie and Myrtle Kay. Mrs. Hansberry, a public schoolteacher, was a great help to her husband in his work.

Translating German and French scholarly manuscripts was one of the many ways she assisted him.

In 1953, Hansberry's dream of studying in Africa finally came true when he was named a Fulbright Research Scholar. In the year that followed, he studied at the University of Cairo and visited more than 100 archaeological sites in Egypt, Ethiopia, the Republic of Sudan, and Rhodesia. He did some digging at some of the sites and added greatly to his knowledge of African history.

Hansberry retired from Howard in 1959. He had always been very popular with the hundreds of African students he taught and helped. In 1952, he had been a co-founder of the African-American Institute. He also helped establish Africa House, a home for African students studying in Washington, and founded the All-African Students Union of the Americas.

Called "Father" by his African students as a mark of respect, Hansberry was honored more widely in Africa than in the United States. One of his former students, Nnamdi Azikiwe, became chancellor of the University of Nigeria. In a letter to Hansberry, Azikiwe wrote: "You initiated me into the sanctuaries of anthropology and ancient African history."[7]

In 1961, the University of Nigeria awarded Hansberry an honorary doctor of letters degree. In 1963, the university established the Hansberry Institute of African Studies in Nsukka, Nigeria; named Hansberry a Distinguished Visiting Professor; and invited him to deliver the institute's inaugural address.

He was also named the first recipient of the Haile Selassie I Prize Trust for pioneering work in African archaeology, history, and anthropology. In the United States, Hansberry was honored with an LL.D. degree from Morgan State College (now Morgan State University) in 1965, and Howard University named a classroom after him in 1972.

Hansberry passed away in Chicago on November 3, 1965. The importance of his pioneering work, proving that Africa possessed an original and highly developed cultural heritage, is still not widely known. Hansberry's publications include several book reviews, magazine articles, and two books: *Pillars in Ethiopian History,* edited by Joseph E. Harris (1981); and *Africa and Africans as Seen by Classical Writers,* edited by Joseph H. Harris (1981).

In spite of the difficulties he encountered in his often lonely struggle, Hansberry loved his life's work and told an interviewer four years before his death: "If I had it to do all over again, I would change nothing. It has been an intensely rewarding life and I would live it as I have."[8]

William Leo Hansberry was greatly respected by Du Bois and other leading scholars. His contributions to the historical profession were perhaps best summed up by his Howard University colleague and former student, Williston H. Lofton, who wrote: "Along with W. E. B. Du Bois and Carter G. Woodson, Hansberry probably did more than any other scholar in these early days to advance the study of the culture and civilization of Africa."[9]

✦

PART FOUR

MODERN TIMES

MOZELL CLARENCE
HILL
(1911–1969)

✦

Mozell Clarence Hill, who would play a significant role in working to end racial segregation in the nation's public schools, was born in Anniston, Alabama, on March 27, 1911.

The youngest of seven children born to Humphrey and Annie Williamson Hill, Clarence grew up in Kansas City, Kansas, and attended city schools. After graduation from high school, he enrolled in the University of Kansas, where he majored in sociology and was awarded a B.A. degree in 1933 and an M.A. degree in 1937.

In 1935, Hill married Marnesba Davis, and the couple had four daughters.

While studying for his master's degree, Hill wrote his thesis on the dynamics of life in the all-black town of Boley, Oklahoma. In later study at the University of Chicago, where he received his Ph.D. degree in 1946, he expanded his study to include six all-black Oklahoma towns.

> ✦ A **thesis** is frequently a long report on major research.

By the early 1900s, there were at least twenty-six of these communities in Oklahoma. Each had been started by people fleeing the harsh racism of the South, joined by smaller numbers of people from the Midwest.

Located about 90 miles southwest of Tulsa, Boley attracted black people who were trying to escape such conditions, own their own land, and control their own lives.

One early resident said of himself and the other pioneers who migrated to what was then Indian Territory (Oklahoma became a state in 1907): "We had covered wagons, and let me tell you, I walked nearly all the way from Louisiana to Oklahoma. . . . We came searchin' for education and freedom."[1]

The mayor of Boley, T. R. Ringe, was born into slavery in Kentucky. The owner of the drugstore, D. J. Turner, grew up among Native Americans in Indian Territory. E. J. Lugrande, a stockholder in one of the banks, migrated from Texas.

Though primarily composed of farmers, the town also attracted black doctors, lawyers, and craftspeople.

Just two years after it was founded, African American educator and Tuskegee Institute President Booker T. Washington paid a visit. He found that the community had already grown to 2,000 residents "with two banks, two cotton-gins, a newspaper, a hotel, and a college, the Creek-Seminole College and Agricultural Institute."[2]

Hill studied most aspects of community life in the six black towns, including the residents' religious and political organizations, economic structures, social relationships, and racial attitudes.

He concluded that the residents had found much of the "moral, industrial and political freedom" they sought, but that this freedom had come at a heavy price: lack of a sufficiently strong economic base for future growth and strongly negative attitudes on the part of the residents toward white people.[3]

In 1937, Hill began teaching sociology at Langston University in

Langston, Oklahoma. The town, which was organized in 1891, was the oldest of Oklahoma's all-black communities. Its residents had donated 40 acres of land to the state so that a black college could be built, and the Oklahoma Territorial Legislature approved such a school in 1897.

Hill taught at Langston University from 1937 to 1946, when he joined the sociology department at Atlanta University.

He stayed at Atlanta until 1958, serving as a professor of sociology, chairman of the department, and editor of the influential *Phylon: The Atlanta University Review of Race and Color.* Many of the students Hill taught at Atlanta and elsewhere went on to earn their doctorates, and they gave him much of the credit for their success.

In some ways, though, his efforts outside the classroom at Atlanta were more important than his efforts inside it. As leader of a community group called the Hungry Club, he helped initiate political and social change in Atlanta through plans made at the club's monthly meetings. The meetings were attended by the leading African Americans in the area, including Whitney Young, M. Carl Holman, Jesse B. Blayton, and the Reverend Martin Luther King Sr.

In 1952 and 1953, Hill visited Great Britain as a lecturer at Cambridge, Manchester, and Edinburgh universities.

By the time he returned to the United States, the issue of school integration had become one of the most controversial and emotionally charged issues in the country.

White resistance to school integration was widespread and often violent, especially in the South, where all of the public schools were segregated. There were also many segregated schools in the North, Midwest, and West, primarily because housing discrimination forced African Americans to live in segregated communities.

Hill's earlier studies about race and class, starting with his research into the all-black towns of Oklahoma, had given him many insights into the causes and possible solutions of racial conflict. As a result of his knowledge, several organizations and communities

THE BATTLE IN THE COURTS

The doctrine of "separate but equal" public accommodations had been established by the U.S. Supreme Court in 1896, in its *Plessy* v. *Ferguson* decision. The decision gave the sanction of the Constitution to racial segregation in education, restaurants, railroads, buses, and all other areas of public life.

"If one race be inferior to the other socially," a majority of the Court wrote, "the Constitution of the United States cannot put them upon the same plane."[4]

In 1937, the constitutionality of racial segregation in a tax-supported school was successfully challenged for the first time. A black man named Donald Murray had been refused admission to the University of Maryland's School of Law because of his race.

Murray's attorney, Thurgood Marshall (who later became a justice of the U.S. Supreme Court), successfully argued for his admittance to the school.

Other challenges to school segregation followed, and in 1954, in its *Brown* v. *Board of Education of Topeka* ruling (Thurgood Marshall was also the lead attorney in this case), the Supreme Court found that racial segregation in public schools was unconstitutional.

asked for his help in resolving conflicts over school integration.

From 1953 to 1955, he was a special research consultant to the Ashmore Project, which was sponsored by the Ford Foundation's Fund for the Advancement of Education. Hill's task was to study the probable course and impact of school integration in the nation.

From 1955 to 1956, in connection with the Knoxville, Tennessee, schools, he helped plan and set up one of the first efforts by a national organization (the Unitarian Service Committee) to bring about peaceful school integration.

From 1955 to 1957, Hill served as co-director of the Georgia Council on Human Relations, and in the early 1960s helped several communities in the New York City area develop school integration plans.

In 1958, he was hired as the first black educator on the faculty of

Columbia University's Teachers College, where he taught the sociology of education.

Hill left Columbia in 1962 to join the faculty of New York University's School of Education, where he served as a professor of educational sociology and anthropology. He remained at the university until he suffered a stroke in 1967.

Mozell Clarence Hill died on March 26, 1969, and was buried in New York City.

He left behind several important publications, including a book titled *Culture of a Contemporary Negro Community* (1943). He was also the author of many articles on race and class.

His most important contributions may well have been the ones he made trying to bring about the peaceful integration of our nation's public schools: contributions that are still needed in many communities.

JAMES P.
COMER, M.D.

(B. 1934)

James Pierpont Comer, who has spent his professional life trying to improve the education of poor and minority children, was born in East Chicago, Indiana, on September 25, 1934. He was the second oldest of three sons and two daughters.

His father, Hugh Comer, had grown up in a poor family in Alabama, then migrated to Indiana where he found work as a laborer in a steel mill. His mother, Maggie Nichols Comer, was from Mississippi and worked as a domestic. She had come north when her stepfather refused to allow her to attend school.

Though neither of James Comer's parents possessed much formal education, they believed passionately in its importance. They passed that passion on to their children. Years later, Comer would recall that his mother often phoned their teachers and never missed a Parent Visitation Day. The family was so poor that young James and his two brothers had to sleep on the pull-out sofa, but the support of their parents helped each succeed in school. Eventually, all five children would go to college, and earn a total of thirteen bachelor and graduate

degrees. The Comers' success in public schools left James with the conviction that children from poor families can do well in school if given proper support and encouragement.

After graduating from East Chicago's Washington High School, Comer attended Indiana University. He excelled in his studies, but it was not easy. Comer recalled, "I had to deal with racial antagonisms. My confidence was shot. . . . That's why I have empathy for black students at every level."[1] He received his A.B. degree from Indiana in 1956, and chose to leave Indiana University and pursue his goal of being a doctor at predominantly black Howard University in Washington, D.C. "I had to go where I was wanted," he said, "not where I was merely tolerated."[2]

In 1959, while attending Howard, Comer married Shirley Ann Arnold. The couple had two children, Brian Jay and Dawn Renee. Comer received his M.D. degree from Howard in 1960 and completed an internship at St. Catherine's Hospital in East Chicago, Indiana, in 1961. While in East Chicago, he worked among the poor and realized that many of their "medical" problems were caused by bad living conditions and feelings of hopelessness.

Returning to Washington, Comer worked with the Public Health Service for two years. He volunteered to help poor people with housing and other problems during his spare time. Wanting to do more than "simply give pills to people who were depressed because of social conditions,"[3] he went back to

A young James Comer is a happy third-year medical student at predominantly black Howard University in 1959.

school and earned a master's degree in public health (M.P.H.) from the University of Michigan in 1964.

By then he had begun to think about "institutions where you could intervene in society and effect some changes for low-income kids. Schools were the natural choice. I decided to become a child psychiatrist, and was accepted at Yale in 1964."[4]

✦ A **psychiatrist** is a doctor who helps people with mental, emotional, and behavioral problems.

Comer completed his training in psychiatry in 1966, and a fellowship program at Yale in 1968. He was then invited to join the staff of the university's Child Study Center as director of a school-intervention project. He accepted the offer and was appointed an assistant professor of psychiatry.

WHY DON'T SOME KIDS DO WELL IN SCHOOL?

"Some kids come from families that often cannot give them the elementary things they need," says Dr. Comer, "like how to say 'Good morning,' 'Thank you,' 'Sit still.'"[5] These students pick up on the feeling of their parents and other adults that they are failures. They may become unruly and threatening to teachers, who in turn become convinced that the children are incapable of learning.

The conflict of "us versus them" between students and teachers then spreads to the parents, and makes the parents angry and frustrated. It also makes it harder for children to learn.

In his book *Maggie's Dream: The Life and Times of a Black Family,* Dr. Comer observes, "When you ask schoolteachers and administrators what is wrong, they say, 'A lack of respect, discipline, motivation.'" They do not take the children's development into account.

"When you ask high school students why they didn't do well in school, or left, the most-often-heard complaint is 'The teachers don't care.'"[6] They do not take the teacher's needs into account.

Comer was delighted to have the opportunity to prove his belief that low-income students could succeed.

When he joined the Child Study Center, Comer began helping parents, teachers, students, administrators, and staff to work together instead of against one another. This approach became known as the Comer Method. He tried the method out in two failing schools in nearby New Haven, Connecticut. Dr. Comer was overjoyed when one of those schools, Martin Luther King Elementary, became among the best in the city.

In 1968, fourth-graders at King Elementary had averaged a year and a half below their grade level in reading and math. By 1979, the school's fourth-grade students were at grade level in both reading and math. Serious disciplinary problems had virtually disappeared. Attendance was way up. The Comer Method had proved its worth.

Comer realizes he still has a long way to go in convincing many educators of the value of his approach. "Even my friends in education still begin by talking curriculum and instruction," he said. "All those things are important, but where's the kid? . . . What's going on with the kid? All of American education has left the development of the child out of it."[7]

Throughout his career, Comer has helped spread his ideas about education through scores of articles in mass-market magazines and professional journals, a monthly column in *Parents*

Dr. James Comer visits with a third-grade class at the Martin Luther King Jr. Elementary School in New Haven, Connecticut.

magazine, several books, and thirty-two chapters in books co-authored with others. He and Dr. Alvin F. Poussaint wrote *Black Child Care*. Comer has also written *Beyond Black and White: Psychological Development* and *School Power: Implications of an Interview Project*.

Comer has served as a consultant on the children's television shows *Sesame Street* and *The Electric Company*.

In addition to his work with children, Comer co-founded the Black Psychiatrists of America (1968) and helped develop the Solomon Fuller Institute in Cambridge, Massachusetts. Named after one of the first African American psychiatrists (Fuller received his M.D. degree from Boston University in 1897), the institute researches mental health issues that relate to black people and develops programs to help train black doctors.

Comer has been a full professor of psychiatry at the Yale Medical School since 1969 and associate dean since 1975. He urges parents to organize their lives around their children, just as his parents did, so that the children can succeed in school and in life.

MAKING A DIFFERENCE

The Comer Method is now being used in more than 450 schools in seventeen states and several foreign countries, often with dramatic results. In the McLeansville Middle School in Guilford Country, North Carolina, the percentage of eighth-graders reading at grade level rose from 65 percent in 1993 to 85 percent in 1997 by using the method.

The method is not perfect. One-third of the schools using it have shown dramatic improvement, one-third have shown slight improvement, and one-third have shown little change.

"If you play baseball those results will put you in the Hall of Fame, and this game's tougher than baseball," Comer said in response to critics.[8]

Marva Delores COLLINS

(B. 1936)

Marva Collins, widely praised for her success in teaching inner-city youths, was born in Monroeville, Alabama, on August 31, 1936. She was the elder of Henry and Bessie Nettles's two daughters.

As a child, Marva could not use the local public library because she was black. But she read everything she could get her hands on: labels on the cans in her father's grocery store, Sunday School stories, the *Farmers' Almanac,* and books her father bought her on trips to Mobile.

Her father's store, she said, "was one of the most challenging and enjoyable classrooms that I would experience, and my father was one of my favorite instructors.[1]

"He spent a great deal of time with me, explaining the business and offering valuable lessons about life and commerce."[2]

Marva's first formal education was in a one-room school where "the teachers were strict and strong; there was no foolishness."[3] She received her high school education at the all-black Escambia County Training School in Atmore, Alabama, where she graduated in 1953.

A Helping Hand

Like many black college students throughout the South, Marva Collins was helped by her church congregation.

"If you went to college in Alabama, you were a celebrity," she said. "The minister had you stand in church and all the people would give you a quarter or fifty cents, or what they could. You didn't get into trouble because in your mind's eye you could see all these people caring about you, depending on you."[4]

Using money she earned doing clerical work for her father, she enrolled in Clark College in Atlanta.

Marva Collins graduated from Clark in 1957 with a B.A. degree in secretarial sciences. Though she had not planned to become a teacher, she accepted a position teaching business subjects at the Monroe County Training School in Alabama.

She said that because her father had taught her "how to survive and have a positive outlook on life, challenges have only intrigued me. Helping others was a natural outgrowth of this attitude; thus teaching was a wonderful choice."[5]

Collins moved to Chicago in 1959 and began working as a medical secretary at Mount Sinai Hospital. In 1960, she met and married Clarence Collins. The couple has three children: Eric Tremayne, Patrick, and Cynthia.

Working at the hospital, Collins realized she "missed the excitement of helping students discover the solution to a problem, of seeing the pieces fit together."[6]

She was determined to return to teaching, but lacked enough education credits for a regular teacher's certificate. So she began substituting full-time in the Chicago school system. Collins taught at the Delano Elementary School for the next fourteen years, and pursued graduate studies at Chicago Teachers College and Columbia University in New York City from 1965 to 1967.

She became increasingly angry at a system in which many teachers came to school unprepared to teach, were disrespectful to their students, and cared little about whether the youngsters learned or not. The children, she declared, "came in and went back out without learning a thing."[7]

Concerned teachers and parents in several cities had started their own schools in the 1960s and 1970s. One of the most successful alternative schools was Harlem Preparatory Academy in New York City, which enrolled hundreds of dropouts from the public school system and sent them on to college.

In 1975, Marva Collins decided to open her own school, using $5,000 from her pension fund. After a brief period conducting the school in the basement of Daniel Hale Williams University, she and her husband built a classroom on the second floor of their home.

She named the school the Westside Preparatory School. Her husband, Charles, took a second job to raise money for supplies and equipment. Collins salvaged books from school trash bins and copied other books by hand. Her first pupils were her daughter and three neighborhood children.

Within three years, Marva Collins had 28 students and a waiting list of 175. Almost all of the children were from low-income families, and many were from families receiving welfare assistance. Believing that all kids can learn if given the opportunity, Collins concentrated on the basics of reading, writing, and mathematics.

Students were required to write a composition every day, memorize a quotation every day, and report on a new book they had read every two weeks. Collins assigned books such as *Aesop's Fables* to five-year-olds, and *Macbeth, Paradise Lost,* and *Uncle Tom's Cabin* to older students.

There were no rigidly structured subjects or class periods. In studying math, for instance, the youngsters also learned about the

A first-grader at a Marva Collins Preparatory School becomes involved in her class when she gets a turn at leading her fellow students in a phonics exercise.

EVERY CHILD CAN LEARN—AND TEACH

"I've seen brilliant kids labeled 'learning disabled' because teachers didn't know what to do with them," Collins said. "The question that always lurks in my mind is, What would I do if this was my child?" Virtually every child can learn, she believes, "if given a little concern and caring."[8]

One of the requirements of the school is that each student has to tutor five other children in the student's neighborhood. Part of the school's motto is "Enter to learn, exit to serve."[9]

Greek and Latin words for mathematical theories, and the life and times of Pythagoras, the Greek mathematician and philosopher.

Collins was interviewed on CBS's *Sixty Minutes* in November 1979 and was the subject of the 1981 CBS television movie *The Marva Collins*

Story, starring Cicely Tyson and Morgan Freeman. Money from the movie helped Collins move her school into two adjoining one-story brick buildings.

The new facilities were home to a staff of 5 teachers and 200 students in kindergarten through the eighth grade, with a waiting list of almost 1,000.

"I don't want to be wealthy," Collins said. "I don't need that kind of power. Power is when I walk into this school and these little kids' eyes hold wonder like a cup."[10]

In 1985, the rock star formerly known as Prince gave Collins a grant to found Westside Prep's National Teacher Training Institute. The institute trains teachers from around the nation to use Collins's methods. She has also written about her methods in *Marva Collins's Way,* co-authored with Civia Tamarkin, and *Ordinary Children, Extraordinary Teachers.*

Collins has won many awards, including one from the United Negro College Fund; the Watson Washburn Award for Excellence in Teaching; Legendary Woman of the World from the city of Birmingham, Alabama; the Fred Hampton Image Award; the Sojourner Truth Award; the Jefferson Award of the American Institute for Public Service; and educator-of-the-year awards from Phi Delta Kappa and the Chicago Urban League.

Honorary doctorates have been presented to her by Howard University, Amherst College, Dartmouth College, Central State University (Ohio), Washington University, and Chicago State University.

Collins's future goals are to establish a day-care center, an adult education facility, and a high school, which she views as a necessity. "Once you get the child together," she declares, "you can get the world together."[11]

JEMISON, M.D.

(B. 1956)

There have always been African Americans who were interested in learning about science, and in teaching other people about its wonders.

One of the first was probably Benjamin Banneker in the eighteenth century. As a child, he lay in the fields at night to learn about the movement of the stars, and eventually taught others about his findings in the almanacs he wrote.

One can only imagine what Banneker would have thought of Dr. Mae Carol Jemison, who rode through the spaces Banneker could only watch from the Maryland farm where he grew up.

Mae C. Jemison, the first African American woman astronaut, was born in Decatur, Alabama, on October 17, 1956. Her parents were Charlie Jemison, a maintenance supervisor, and Dorothy Jemison, an elementary school teacher. Mae was the youngest of their three children.

The family moved to Chicago when Mae was only three years old, and she was educated in Chicago's public schools. An uncle who was

a social worker introduced her to the world of science when she was four, helping her develop an interest in astronomy, archaeology, and anthropology that she pursued throughout her childhood.

Like Benjamin Banneker, she said she "used to lie outside on a summer's night and stare up at the stars . . . [and] wonder what the stars were, what they were made of."[1]

Mae graduated from Morgan Park High School in 1973 with a National Achievement Scholarship to Stanford University in California. She was confident she could succeed in any field because her parents had taught her to maintain "the confidence and creativity and motivation that every child, each one of us, is born with."[2]

Mae was only sixteen when she entered Stanford. She graduated in 1977 with two degrees: a B.S. in chemical engineering and a B.A. in African American studies. She next enrolled in the Cornell University Medical College, because she was determined to become a doctor. During her years at Cornell, Jemison joined the American Student Medical Association, which helped her to travel and study in Cuba.

She also treated refugees at a camp in Cambodia and, with the help of the African Medical and Research Foundation, took part in health studies in Kenya.

Jemison received her M.D. degree from Cornell in 1981, and served her internship at the Los Angeles County/University of Southern California Medical Center in 1982.

Her experiences among the sick and malnourished people she helped in Cuba, Cambodia, and Kenya must have affected her deeply, for she volunteered to serve as a medical officer in the Peace Corps in Africa. From 1983 to 1985, Jemison worked in Sierra Leone and Liberia, giving medical care to Peace Corps volunteers and U.S. embassy personnel.

Always interested in educating others, she began teaching volunteers. She also wrote self-care manuals, and developed guidelines for health volunteers on safety and public health issues. Then she returned to the United States to work as a general practitioner at CIGNA Health Plans of California, a health maintenance organization.

During all these years, she still remembered the awe she had felt as a child looking at the stars, and dreamed of one day going into outer space.

In 1985, while working as a general practitioner and studying engineering at night at the University of California, Jemison applied to the National Aeronautics and Space Administration (NASA) to become an astronaut. Three months later, NASA suspended its astronaut acceptance program after the space shuttle *Challenger* exploded shortly after liftoff.

Jemison applied again when the program was resumed, and on June 4, 1987, received word that she had been selected for astronaut

EXPLORING THE HEAVENS

Like most astronauts, Jemison had to wait several years to go into space. But on September 12, 1992, she and six other astronauts blasted off from the Kennedy Space Center in Florida, aboard the shuttle *Endeavor*.

"I had this big smile on my face," she said of that day. "I was so excited. This is what I had wanted to do for a very long time. . . . It was the realization of many, many dreams of many people."[3]

Among the items she took with her was a poster from the Alvin Ailey American Dance Theater, depicting the dance *Cry*. Jemison explained to the company's director, Judith Jamison, that she took the poster into space because the dance was created for "all black women everywhere."[4]

When some people expressed the belief that Jemison's achievements as an astronaut did nothing to help black people, she replied: "I take that as an affront. It presupposes that black people have never been involved in exploring the heavens, but this is not so. Ancient African empires—Mali, Songhai, Egypt—had scientists, astronomers. The fact is that space and its resources belong to all of us, not to any one group."[5]

training. She was one of 15 chosen out of approximately 2,000 applicants. Jemison joined NASA's space program in 1987. By the summer of 1988, she had completed the agency's one-year training and evaluation program, and qualified as a mission specialist.

In 1993, she resigned from NASA to found the Jemison Group, Inc. Among the group's projects are a satellite-based telecommunications system to help bring health care to countries in West Africa.

Jemison believes in education for the entire planet. Another of her projects is an international science camp called The Earth We Share. The camp has an experimental curriculum and is for students between the ages of twelve and sixteen.

"Every child comes into this world curious about things," she said. "They're picking up bugs, and slime, and fuzz out of the couch, trying to figure out what's going on. . . . But what happens when they go into the classroom? We have this idea that if you just tell people to memorize something by rote, then it's going to hit and stick; and we all know that's not true. We all learn by doing."[6]

She is also interested in trying to figure out "how we can use advanced technologies in developing countries. . . . For example, malaria is a very difficult disease to create a vaccine for. . . . But yet it would make a very big difference to the lives of people in developing countries."[7]

The educator/doctor/scientist/astronaut is currently a professor of environmental studies at Dartmouth College in Hanover, New Hampshire. She has received many awards in her career, including the *Essence* Science and Technology Award (1988), the Gamma Sigma Gamma Woman of the Year Award (1989), and the *Ebony* Black Achievement Award (1992).

For Jemison, the words "I think, I wonder and I understand"[8] are at the heart of science, just as they were at the heart of her childhood determination to gain knowledge of the world around her and use that knowledge to improve the world.

Chronology

1731	Benjamin Banneker born
1776	Revolutionary War begins
1780	Daniel Coker born
1779	Catherine (Katy) Ferguson born
1783	Revolutionary War ends
1792	Benjamin Banneker publishes his first almanac
1795	Alexander Lucius Twilight born
1806	Benjamin Banneker dies
	Sarah Mapps Douglass born
1812	The War of 1812
1823	Mary Smith Peake born
	Alexander Lucius Twilight graduates from Middlebury College. He is the first black college graduate in the United States.
1829	Peter Humphries Clark born
1830	Abolitionists organize the Underground Railroad
1834	Patrick Francis Healy born
1846	Daniel Coker dies
1837	Charlotte Forten Grimké born
	Francis Louis Cardozo born
	Cheyney University of Pennsylvania (formerly Cheyney State College) founded
1840	James Milton Turner born
1848	Susie King Taylor born
1850	Of the nearly 400,000 free blacks in the United States, 3,000 own land
1854	Catherine (Katy) Ferguson dies
	Lincoln University, Pennsylvania, founded
1856	Booker Taliaferro Washington born
	Wilberforce University, Ohio, founded
1857	In the case of *Scott* v. *Sanford*, the U.S. Supreme Court rules against citizenship for blacks
	Alexander Lucius Twilight dies
1861	Civil War begins
1862	Mary Smith Peake dies

1863	Emancipation Proclamation issued by President Abraham Lincoln frees all slaves in the Confederate states
	Fifty-fourth Massachusetts Volunteer Regiment mustered into service
	Fifty-fourth Massachusetts Volunteer Regiment assaults Fort Wagner, South Carolina
	Mary Church Terrell born
1864	George Washington Carver born
1865	Civil War ends
	President Lincoln assassinated
1866	James Milton Turner establishes Lincoln Institute in Jefferson City, Missouri.
1867	Congress passes the first Reconstruction Act, requiring former Confederate states to ratify the "Civil War Amendments," write new constitutions, and grant voting rights to all males, regardless of "race, color, or previous condition of servitude."
	Congress passes the Thirteenth Amendment, abolishing slavery in the United States; it is later ratified
	Talladega College, Alabama, founded
	Fisk University, Tennessee, founded
	Howard University founded in Washington, D.C.
	Robert Russa Moton born
1868	Howard University College of Medicine, the first medical school to admit blacks, founded in Washington, D.C.
	Hampton Institute, Virginia, founded
	John Hope born
	William Edward Burghardt Du Bois born
1869	Tougaloo College, Mississippi, founded
1874	Patrick Francis Healey becomes president of Georgetown College (later Georgetown University)
1875	Mary McLeod Bethune born
	Carter Godwin Woodson born
1877	Reconstruction ends
1881	Booker Taliaferro Washington founds Tuskegee Institute, Alabama
1882	Sarah Mapps Douglass dies
1890	Mordecai Wyatt Johnson born
1894	William Leo Hansberry born
1896	In the case of *Plessy* v. *Ferguson*, the U.S. Supreme Court rules that "separate but equal" facilities for blacks are constitutional

1898	Spanish-American War
1902	Susie King Taylor publishes her autobiography, *Reminiscences of My Life in Camp: A Black Woman's Civil War Memoirs*
1903	Francis Louis Cardozo dies
1904	Mary McLeod Bethune opens her school, which merges with Cookman College in 1922 to become Bethune-Cookman College
1905	Du Bois, Terrell, and Hope attend the meeting of the Niagra Movement, forerunner of the National Association for the Advancement of Colored People
1906	John Hope becomes president of Atlanta Baptist College (renamed Morehouse College in 1913)
1909	National Association for the Advancement of Colored People founded
1910	Patrick Francis Healy dies
	W. E. B. Du Bois becomes editor of *The Crisis* magazine
1911	Mozell Clarence Hill born
1912	Susie King Taylor dies
1914	World War I begins in Europe
	Charlotte Forten Grimké dies
1915	James Milton Turner dies
	Booker Taliaferro Washington dies
	Robert Russa Moton becomes principal of Tuskegee Institute
1917	United States enters World War I
1918	World War I ends
1925	Peter Humphries Clark dies
1926	Mordecai Wyatt Johnson becomes first black president of Howard University
1929	Stock market crash ushers in the Great Depression
1934	James Pierpont Comer born
1936	Marva Delores Collins born
	John Hope dies
1939	World War II begins in Europe
1940	Robert Russa Moton dies
1941	United States enters World War II
	The Great Depression ends
1943	George Washington Carver dies
	United Negro College Fund proposed by Dr. Frederick Patterson
1945	World War II ends

1950	Carter Godwin Woodson dies
	Korean War begins
1953	Korean War ends
1954	In the case of *Brown* v. *Board of Education of Topeka*, the U.S. Supreme Court rules that "separate but equal" schools are unconstitutional and orders integration "with all deliberate speed"
	Mary Church Terrell dies
1955	Mary McLeod Bethune dies
1956	Mae Carol Jemison, M.D., born
1963	Martin Luther King Jr. tells the March on Washington, "I have a dream."
	W. E. B. Du Bois dies
1964	Congress passes a Civil Rights Act, ending federal funding of segregated hospitals and schools
	America enters the Vietnam War
1965	William Leo Hansberry dies
1969	Mozell Clarence Hill dies
1972	United Negro College Fund adopts the slogan, "A Mind Is a Terrible Thing to Waste"
1973	Vietnam War ends
1975	Marva Collins opens the Westside Preparatory School
1976	Mordecai Wyatt Johnson dies
1990	The Rockefeller Foundation funds the Comer Method
1992	Mae Carol Jemison goes into space aboard the shuttle *Endeavor*

NOTES

INTRODUCTION

1. Frederick Douglass, *Life and Times of Frederick Douglass* (New York: Bonanza Books, 1962), 79.

2. Gerda Lerner, ed., *Black Women in White America: A Documentary History* (New York: Vintage Books, 1972), 139.

3. Herbert Aptheker, *A Documentary History of the Negro People in the United States*, vol. 1 (New York: Citadel Press Book, 1952), 298.

BENJAMIN BANNEKER

1. Rev. William J. Simmons, *Men of Mark: Eminent, Progressive and Rising* (New York: Arno Press and The New York Times Company, 1968), 344.

2. Silvio A. Bedini, *The Life of Benjamin Banneker* (New York: Charles Scribner's & Sons, 1972), 40.

3. Ibid., 122.

4. Ibid., 153.

5. Sidney Kaplan and Emma Nogrady Kaplan, *The Black Presence in the Era of the American Revolution* (Amherst: University of Massachusetts Press, 1989), 145.

CATHERINE (KATY) FERGUSON

1. "Catherine Ferguson, Black Founder of a Sunday-School," *Negro History Bulletin* (December 1972), 176.

2. Walter Wilson, ed., *The Selected Writings of W. E. B. Du Bois* (New York: A Mentor Book, 1970), 97.

3. Ibid., 97.

DANIEL COKER

1. Sidney Kaplan and Emma Nogrady Kaplan, *The Black Presence in the Era of the American Revolution* (Amherst: University of Massachusetts Press, 1989), 209.

2. Rayford W. Logan and Michael R. Winston, eds., *Dictionary of American Negro Biography* (New York: W.W. Norton & Company, 1982), 120.

ALEXANDER LUCIUS TWILIGHT

1. "The Iron-willed Black Schoolmaster and His Granite Academy," *Middlebury College News Letter* (Spring 1974), 8.

SARAH MAPPS DOUGLASS

1. Sidney Kaplan and Emma Nogrady Kaplan, *The Black Presence in the Era of the American Revolution* (Amherst: University of Massachusetts Press, 1989), 100.

MARY SMITH PEAKE

1. Rayford W. Logan and Michael R. Winston, eds., *Dictionary of American Negro Biography* (New York: W.W. Norton & Company, 1982), 486.

2. W. Augustus Low, ed., *Encyclopedia of Black America* (New York: McGraw-Hill Book Company, 1981), 462.

P E T E R H U M P H R I E S C L A R K

1. Herbert Aptheker, *A Documentary History of the Negro People in the United States*, vol. 1 (New York: Citadel Press, 1951), 345.

2. Rayford W. Logan and Michael R. Winston, eds., *Dictionary of American Negro Biography* (1864; reprint, New York: W.W. Norton & Company, 1982), 115.

3. Peter H. Clark, *The Black Brigade of Cincinnati* (New York: Arno Press and The New York Times Company, 1969), iv.

P A T R I C K F R A N C I S H E A L Y

1. Albert S. Foley, *God's Men of Color* (New York: Arno Press and The New York Times Company, 1969), 25.

C H A R L O T T E F O R T E N G R I M K É

1. William E. B. Du Bois, James Weldon Johnson, and Booker T. Washington, *Three Negro Classics* (New York: Avon Books, 1965), 234.

2. "A Social Experiment: The Port Royal Journal of Charlotte L. Forten, 1862–1863," *Journal of Negro History* (July 1950), 242.

3. Gerda Lerner, ed., *Black Women in White America: A Documentary History* (New York: Vintage Books, 1973), 96.

4. Ibid.

5. Rayford W. Logan and Michael R. Winston, eds., *Dictionary of American Negro Biography* (New York: W.W. Norton & Company, 1982), 234.

6. "A Social Experiment," 259–60.

F R A N C I S L O U I S C A R D O Z O

1. "The South as It Is," *The Nation* (1865), 779.

2. W. E. B. Du Bois, *Black Reconstruction in America* (New York: Atheneum, 1975), 396.

J A M E S M I L T O N T U R N E R

1. "James Milton Turner: A Little Known Benefactor of His People," *Journal of Negro History* (October 1934), 375.

2. Ibid., 377.

3. Ibid., 378.

4. Ibid., 406.

5. Ibid.

6. Ibid., 411.

S U S I E K I N G T A Y L O R

1. Susie King Taylor, *Reminiscences of My Life in Camp* (New York: Arno Press and The New York Times Company, 1968), 5.

2. Ibid., 9.

3. Ibid., 8–9.

4. Ibid., 21.

5. Joseph T. Wilson, *The Black Phalanx* (Salem, N.H.: Ayer Company Publishers, Inc., 1992), 504–505.

6. Ibid., 505.

7. Taylor, *Reminiscences*, 54.

8. Ibid., 67.

BOOKER T. WASHINGTON

1. William E. B. Du Bois, James Weldon Johnson, and Booker T. Washington, *Three Negro Classics* (New York: Avon Books, 1965), 44–45.

2. Ibid., 51.

3. Ibid., 68.

4. Ibid., 87.

5. Ibid., 108.

6. Ibid., 149.

7. Ibid., 252.

MARY CHURCH TERRELL

1. Paula Giddings, *When and Where I Enter* (New York: William Morrow and Co., 1984), 109.

2. Gerda Lerner, ed., *Black Women in White America: A Documentary History* (New York: Vintage Books, 1973), 211.

3. William Loren Katz, *Eyewitness* (New York: Touchstone, 1995), 336.

ROBERT RUSSA MOTON

1. Lerone Bennett Jr., *The Shaping of Black America* (New York: Penguin Books, 1975), 211.

2. Rayford W. Logan and Michael R. Winston, eds., *Dictionary of American Negro Biography* (New York: W.W. Norton & Company, 1982), 469.

3. Logan and Winston, *Dictionary of American Negro Biography*, 460.

JOHN HOPE

1. Rayford W. Logan and Michael R. Winston, eds., *Dictionary of American Negro Biography* (New York: W.W. Norton & Company, 1982), 321.

2. Ibid., 322.

3. Ibid.

4. Lerone Bennett Jr., *The Shaping of Black America* (New York: Penguin Books, 1975), 285.

5. Logan and Winston, *Dictionary of Negro Biography*, 324.

W. E. B. DU BOIS

1. Walter Wilson, ed., *The Selected Writings of W. E. B. Du Bois* (New York: A Mentor Book, 1970), 255.

2. Lerone Bennett Jr., *Pioneers in Protest* (Chicago: Johnson Publishing Company Inc., 1968), 246.

3. Ibid., 248.

4. Ibid., 242.

5. Rayford W. Logan and Michael R. Winston, eds., *Dictionary of American Negro Biography* (New York: W.W. Norton & Company, 1982), 195.

6. Bennett, *Pioneers in Protest*, 249.

7. Ibid., 250–51.

8. Wilson, *Selected Writings of W. E. B. Du Bois*, 102–103.

9. Logan and Winston, *Dictionary of American Negro Biography*, 198.

MARY McLEOD BETHUNE

1. Gerda Lerner, ed., *Black Women in White America: A Documentary History* (New York: Vintage Books, 1973), 135.

2. Ibid., 136.

3. Ibid.

4. Ibid.

5. Ibid., 137.

6. Ibid.

7. Ibid., 139.

8. Madeline Stratton, *Negroes Who Helped Build America* (Boston: Ginn and Company, 1965), 82.

9. Ibid.

10. Lerner, *Black Women in White America*, 142.

11. Stratton, *Negroes Who Helped Build America*, 87.

12. "My Last Will and Testament," *Ebony* (November 1973), 84–86.

CARTER G. WOODSON

1. "The Unfinished Business of Carter G. Woodson," *City Sun*, March 20–26, 1991, 31.

2. Anna Rothe, ed., *Current Biography 1944* (New York: H.W. Wilson Company, 1944), 743.

MORDECAI WYATT JOHNSON

1. Edwin R. Embree, *13 Against the Odds* (New York: Viking Press, 1944), 182.

2. Rayford W. Logan, *Howard University: The First Hundred Years, 1867–1967* (New York: New York University Press, 1969), 249.

3. Embree, *13 Against the Odds*, 184.

4. Ibid., 186.

5. Logan, *Howard University*, 251.

6. Ibid., 250.

7. Ibid., 449.

8. "Preacher and Ex-House Whip Enjoys New Pulpit," *New York Times*, October 9, 1991, B9.

9. Charles M. Christian, ed., *Black Saga: The African American Experience* (New York: Houghton Mifflin Company, 1995), 561.

WILLIAM LEO HANSBERRY

1. Joseph E. Harris, ed., *Pillars in Ethiopian History*, vol. 1 (Washington, D.C.: Howard University Press, 1981), 4.

2. "Unsung Howard U. Professor Is World's Best African Authority," *Ebony* (February 1961), 65–66.

3. Harris, *Pillars in Ethiopian History,* vol. 1, 6.

4. Ibid., 8.

5. "Unsung Howard U. Professor Is World's Best African Authority," 60.

6. Harris, *Pillars in Ethiopian History,* vol. 1, 27–28.

7. Ibid., 3.

8. "Unsung Howard U. Professor Is World's Best African Authority," 68.

9. Harris, *Pillars in Ethiopian History,* vol. 1, 3.

MOZELL CLARENCE HILL

1. "The All-Negro Communities of Oklahoma: The Natural History of a Social Movement," *Journal of Negro History* (July 1946), 258.

2. Charles M. Christian, ed., *Black Saga: The African Amercian Experience* (New York: Houghton Mifflin Company, 1995), 294.

3. Ibid.

4. Ibid., 282.

JAMES P. COMER

1. Charles Moritz, ed., *Current Biography Yearbook 1991* (New York: H.W. Wilson Company, 1991), 149.

2. James P. Comer, *Beyond Black and White* (New York: Quadrangle Books, 1972), 149.

3. Moritz, *Current Biography Yearbook 1991,* 149.

4. Ibid.

5. Ibid.

6. Ibid., 150.

7. "Pleading a Case for the Child," *New York Times,* July 1, 1998, B8.

8. Ibid., B1.

MARVA DELORES COLLINS

1. "The Love that Changed My Life," *Ebony* (May 1990), 38.

2. Ibid.

3. Charles Moritz, ed., *Current Biography Yearbook 1986* (New York: H.W. Wilson Company, 1986), 95.

4. Darlene Clark Hine, ed., *Black Women in America* (New York: Carlson Publishing Inc., 1993), 266.

5. Moritz, *Current Biography Yearbook 1986,* 95.

6. Ibid.

7. "Teacher," *People* (December 11, 1978), 89.

8. Brian Lanker, *I Dream a World* (New York: Stewart, Tabori & Chang, 1989), 75.

9. "EssenceWomen," *Essence* (January 1979), 29.

10. Lanker, *I Dream a World,* 75.

11. "EssenceWomen," 29.

MAE CAROL JEMISON, M.D.

1. "National Press Club Luncheon Speaker: Astronaut Mae Jemison" (Washington, D.C.: Federal News Service Transcript, April 19, 1998), 5.

2. Ibid.

3. Judith Graham, ed., *Current Biography Yearbook 1993* (New York: H.W. Wilson Company, 1993), 280.

4. Darlene Clark Hine, *Black Women in America* (New York: Carlson Publishing Inc., 1993), 634.

5. Graham, *Current Biography Yearbook 1993*, 280.

6. "National Press Club Luncheon Speaker: Astronaut Mae Jemison," 10.

7. Ibid., 18.

8. Ibid., 9.

BIBLIOGRAPHY

BOOKS FOR ADULTS

Aptheker, Herbert. *A Documentary History of the Negro People in the United States*, vol. 1. New York: Citadel Press, 1951.

Bedini, Silvio A. *The Life of Benjamin Banneker*. New York: Charles Scribner & Sons, 1972.

Bennett, Lerone Jr. *Pioneers in Protest*. Chicago: Johnson Publishing Company, 1968.

————. *The Shaping of Black America*. New York: Penguin Books, 1975.

Christian, Charles M., ed. *Black Saga: The African American Experience*. New York: Houghton Mifflin, 1995.

Clark, Peter H. *The Black Brigade of Cincinnati*. New York: Arno Press and The New York Times Company, 1969.

Comer, James P. *Beyond Black and White*. New York: Quadrangle Books, 1972.

Douglass, Frederick. *Life and Times of Frederick Douglass*. New York: Bonanza Books, 1962.

Du Bois, W. E. B. *Black Reconstruction in America*. New York: Atheneum, 1975.

Du Bois, W. E. B., James Weldon Johnson, and Booker T. Washington. *Three Negro Classics*. New York: Avon Books, 1965.

Embree, Edwin R. *13 Against the Odds*. New York: Viking Press, 1944.

Foley, Albert S. *God's Men of Color*. New York: Arno Press and The New York Times Company, 1969.

Franklin, John Hope. *From Slavery to Freedom: A History of Negro Americans*. New York: Alfred Knopf, 1980.

Giddings, Paula. *When and Where I Enter*. New York: William Morrow, 1984.

Harris, Joseph, ed. *Pillars in Ethiopian History*, vol. 1. Washington, D.C.: Howard University Press, 1981.

Kaplan, Sidney, and Emma Nogrady Kaplan, eds. *The Black Presence in the Era of the American Revolution*. Amherst: University of Massachusetts Press, 1989.

Katz, William Loren. *Eyewitness: A Living Documentary of the African American Contribution to American History*. New York: Touchstone, 1995.

Lanker, Brian. *I Dream a World*. New York: Stewart, Tabori & Chang, 1986.

Lerner, Gerda, ed. *Black Women in White America: A Documentary History*. New York: Vintage Books, 1973.

Logan, Rayford W. *Howard University: The First Hundred Years, 1867–1967*. Washington, D.C.: Howard University Press, 1968.

Logan, Rayford W., and Michael R. Winston, eds. *Dictionary of American Negro Biography*. New York: W.W. Norton, 1982.

Simmons, Rev. William J. *Men of Mark: Eminent, Progressive and Rising*. New York: Arno Press and The New York Times Company, 1968.

Taylor, Susie King. *Reminiscences of My Life in Camp*. New York: Arno Press and The New York Times Company, 1968.

Wilson, Joseph T. *The Black Phalanx.* Salem, N.H.: Ayer Company Publishers, 1992.

Wilson, Walter, ed. *The Selected Writings of W. E. B. Du Bois* New York: A Mentor Book, 1970.

FOR YOUNG READERS

Stratton, Madeline. *Negroes Who Helped Build America.* Boston: Ginn and Company, 1965.

ARTICLES

Billiard, lrving. "James Milton Turner: A Little Known Benefactor of His People." *Journal of Negro History* (October 1934): 372–411.

Comer, James P. "Are We Failing Our Children?" *Ebony* (August 1974): 54.

Crawford, Mark. "Unsung Howard U. Professor Is World's Best African Authority." *Ebony* (February 1961): 58–68.

Forten, Charlotte L. "A Social Experiment: The Port Royal Journal of Charlotte L. Forten, 1862–1863." *Journal of Negro History* (July 1950): 233–264.

Hartvik, Alien. "Catherine Ferguson, Black Founder of a Sunday-school." *Negro History Bulletin* (December 1972): 176.

Hill, Mozell Clarence. "The All-Negro Communities of Oklahoma: The Natural History of a Social Movement." *Journal of Negro History* (July 1946): 258.

"The Iron-willed Black Schoolmaster and His Granite Academy." *Middlebury College News Letter* (Spring 1974): 6–14.

Jackson, L. P. "The Origin of Hampton Institute." *Journal of Negro History* (April 1925): 131–149.

Logan, Rayford W. "Carter G. Woodson: Mirror and Molder of His Time, 1875–1950." *Journal of Negro History* (January 1973): 1–17.

"The Love that Changed My Life." *Ebony* (May 1990): 38.

Marshall, Marilyn. "Child of the '60s Set to Become First Black Woman in Space." *Ebony* (August 1989): 50–55.

"The South as It Is." *The Nation* (1865): 779.

PICTURE CREDITS

Pages 6 and 10, courtesy of the Library of Congress, Washington, D.C.; page 13, courtesy of Photographs and Print Division, Schomburg Center for Research in Black Culture, the New York Public Library/Astor, Lenox and Tilden Foundations; page 17: courtesy of Association for the Study of African American Life and History, Silver Spring, Md.; page 19: courtesy of Photographs and Print Division, Schomburg Center for Research in Black Culture, the New York Public Library/Astor, Lenox and Tilden Foundations; page 22: courtesy of Special Collections, Middlebury College, Middlebury, Vt.; page 30: courtesy of Library of Congress, Washington, D.C.; page 35: public domain; page 36: courtesy of Library of Congress, Washington, D.C.; page 39: courtesy of Photographs and Print Division, Schomburg Center for Research in Black Culture, the New York Public Library/Astor, Lenox and Tilden Foundations; page 43: courtesy of Library of Congress, Washington, D.C.; page 47: courtesy of Moorland-Spingarn Research Center, Howard University, Washington, D.C.; pages 48 and 53, courtesy of Library of Congress, Washington, D.C.; page 59: courtesy of Photographs and Print Division, Schomburg Center for Research in Black Culture, the New York Public Library/Astor, Lenox and Tilden Foundations; page 64: courtesy of Moorland-Spingarn Research Center, Howard University, Washington, D.C.; pages 72 and 75, courtesy of Library of Congress, Washington, D.C.; page 76: courtesy of Photographs and Print Division, Schomburg Center for Research in Black Culture, the New York Public Library/Astor, Lenox and Tilden Foundations; page 79: courtesy of Library of Congress, Washington, D.C.; page 85: courtesy of Photographs and Print Division, Schomburg Center for Research in Black Culture, the New York Public Library/Astor, Lenox and Tilden Foundations; page 88: courtesy of Library of Congress, Washington, D.C.; page 91: courtesy of Moorland-Spingarn Research Center, Howard University, Washington, D.C.; page 97: courtesy of Library of Congress, Washington, D.C.; page 100: courtesy of Photographs and Print Division, Schomburg Center for Research in Black Culture, the New York Public Library/Astor, Lenox and Tilden Foundations; page 104: courtesy of Library of Congress, Washington, D.C.; page 111: courtesy of National Archives, Washington, D.C.; page 116: courtesy of Moorland-Spingarn Research Center, Howard University, Washington, D.C.; page 118: courtesy of Howard University Archives, Washington, D.C.; page 120: courtesy of the United Negro College Fund Communications Office; page 123: courtesy of Moorland-Spingarn Research Center, Howard University, Washington, D.C.; page 132: courtesy of Oklahoma Historical Society, Oklahoma City; pages 138, 139, and 141, courtesy of James Comer, M.D.; pages 144 and 147, courtesy of the *Milwaukee Journal Sentinel;* page 150: courtesy of UPI/Corbis-Bettmann.

INDEX